Making a living from old shoes

Tanzanian street vendors as urban experts

Imprint

The Deutsche Nationalbibliothek lists this publication in the Deutsche Nationalbibliografie; detailed bibliographic data are available on the Internet at http://dnb.dnb.de

ISBN 978-3-7165-1826-7

© 2016 Benteli, imprint of bnb media gmbh, Zurich, and Ethnographic Museum at the University of Zurich

www.benteli.ch

The work is copyright protected. Any use outside of the close boundaries of the copyright law, which has not been granted permission by the publisher, is unauthorized and liable for prosecution. This especially applies to duplications, translations, microfilming, and any saving or processing in electronic systems.

1st edition 2016

Editor: Mareile Flitsch
Authors: Alexis Malefakis, Christa Luginbühl, Tabea Grob
Graphic concept: Kathrin Leuenberger
Bibliography: Agnes Kovacs
English translation: Alexis Malefakis, Helen Gimber, Tabea Grob
Copyediting: Helen Rana
Picture rights: Owned by the persons and institutions listed in the picture credentials

All of the information in this volume has been compiled to the best of the editors'/authors' knowledge. The publisher assumes no responsibility for its accuracy or completeness as well as copyright discrepancies and refers to the specified sources. All rights to the photographs are property of the photographer (please refer to the picture credits).

Alexis Malefakis   Christa Luginbühl   Tabea Grob

Making a living from old shoes
Tanzanian street vendors as urban experts

Mareile Flitsch (ed.)
Ethnographic Museum at the University of Zurich

BENTELI

Content

Foreword

Imagine that you bought a pair of shoes, wore them for a while, and eventually discarded them in one of the usual charity collection bins in your neighbourhood, believing that you were doing something charitable and being unaware that the shoes were, in fact, being fed into a gigantic market in which the final retailers earned the least. Imagine then that you travelled to Dar es Salaam in Tanzania, East Africa, where you encountered a young man who tried to persuade you to buy a pair of shoes – and you recognised those very same shoes in his hands, refurbished and looking as good as new. Who or what would actually be meeting in that instant? The so-called 'first' and 'third' worlds? A Western consumer and developing world peddler? Donor and recipient? Affluence and poverty? Europe and Africa? We consumers of brand new shoes are worlds apart from African shoe vendors.

Anthropology claims to observe the world through the eyes of actors in different cultural contexts. We learn local languages and find out about everyday life through participant observation, because we are interested in understanding the perspectives that people have on their own life worlds. Anthropology is about acknowledging contemporaneity,[1] appreciating the fact that people everywhere in the world confront their everyday lives in a conscious and informed way, orienting themselves in the world as intelligent human beings. We are all living at the same moment in time, but dispersed over different places and under different circumstances which are, nowadays, globally interrelated in peculiar ways. One such way is the potential to find our own discarded shoes being sold on a street in Dar es Salaam.

Some years ago, I heard a talk by the German-Greek anthropologist Alexis Malefakis at the Lebewohlfabrik Cultural Centre, which was organised by the Zurich Ethnological Association. Alexis described his fieldwork with a group of shoe vendors in Tanzania. He explained that he had learned Swahili, then become an apprentice with rural migrants in Dar es Salaam, joining them in their business, learning about their world views and their approach to the city. Together with them, he had sought answers to the question, what do Europe's discarded shoes mean for people on the African continent?

He found that what the shoe vendors in Dar es Salaam accomplish is not just bricolage, shrewd improvisation for the sake of survival in poverty, not merely an informal economy. Living in desperate conditions in their home villages had spurred those young men on to take the initiative in a specific way. They had established a niche for themselves in the urban jungle of global economic entanglements and market dictates, utilising their social, economic and material-technological competences and skills to the utmost, by selling second-hand shoes brought ashore in Dar es Salaam from the container economy of the Indian Ocean. They did so by establishing a market that only exists as an ephemeral event – momentary encounters in the streets which cease to exist the instant that a conversation or transaction ends. The more you learn about their methods and forms of organisation, the more you marvel at their accomplishments.

Alexis Malefakis is now curator of the African collections at the Ethnographic Museum at the University of Zurich, and he submitted an ethnography on street vendors in Tanzania as his doctoral dissertation in 2014.

With the exhibition catalogue, *Making a living from old shoes: Tanzanian street vendors as urban experts*, he provides a book that will hopefully inspire many young anthropologists. As he shows here, it is well worth focusing your attention on something so seemingly banal as patched and prettied-up shoes, that it is a worthwhile endeavour to 'follow the shoe',[2] if you know how to ask the right questions.

The answers to these questions prompt us to understand and respect the people who are occupied with acting as prudent professionals, dismantling and recycling the remnants of our consumerist society. In the final analysis, this means that we need to rethink our own consumer behaviour, as well as our relationship to the Global South more generally.

As anthropology's 'showcase', we are particularly keen to make the results of our research projects publicly available via exhibitions, publications and events. For this purpose, we always like to involve researchers and experts from other subject areas and institutions, and to include talented students within our projects. Christa Luginbühl of the Berne Decleration (BD), who is the national coordinator of the Clean Clothes Campaign (CCC) in Switzerland, contributes a thoroughly researched insight into the global processes of shoe production and offers some recommendations on how we, as consumers, can contribute to fairer trade in clothes and shoes. Tabea Grob, an anthropology student at the University of Zurich, provides the findings from her research into the role that old clothes play as a global commodity. These sections complement Alexis Malefakis' ethnographic chapters on the everyday work and life of street vendors in Tanzania. This book was developed in cooperation with Benteli Publishers to accompany the exhibition *Making a living from old shoes*, an exhibition that also comprises innovative methods of communicating research results. The exhibition not only includes the shoes and tools that the shoe vendors used, along with photographs and videos from Tanzania – but also has a thought-provoking computer game that allows visitors to directly experience the working conditions of the shoe vendors themselves.

I thank Christa Luginbühl and Tabea Grob, as well as Alexis Malefakis and Markus Sebastian Braun from Benteli Publishers, for their commitment to this publication.

Zurich, February 2016
Mareile Flitsch

---

1 Fabian 1983.
2 Marcus 1995.

Alexis Malefakis

The world in a shoe: an introduction

"If, in a shoe, there is a label that says 'Made in Germany', I can sell it for a high price. People say things from Germany are good quality. Shoes 'Made in Italy' or 'Made in Brazil' are very popular as well. And even shoes 'Made in China' can be sold for a lot, if they have been worn in Europe first. Because the Chinese produce shoes of two different qualities: the high quality that goes to Europe, and the low quality and the fake brands that we get in the shops here in Africa. I can explain to a customer that a shoe may be 'Made in China' but, because it was bought and worn in Europe first, it is still an 'original'!"[1]

Today, no anthropological inquiry into a local life world can ignore the economic, political and cultural influences of various global dynamics. Even in regions that may appear remote to the European onlooker, people's lives are often shaped in significant ways by ideas, commodities, consumption patterns and practices that come from other parts of the world. In contrast to the classical period of anthropology around the turn of the 19th and 20th centuries, when an isolated 'tribe' was considered the ideal unit of analysis to study aboriginal peoples unaffected by Western civilisation, nowadays anthropological studies increasingly focus on global *flows* of goods, people, ideas and media images and their interplay with local world views and everyday experiences.[2] In that sense, the everyday life of the group of street vendors in Tanzania that this book mainly focuses on is organised around a commodity that is inscribed with various global connections.

Firstly, the ladies' shoes that this particular group of street vendors specialises in originally come from Asia, the USA and Europe, and therefore have already travelled a long distance before arriving at Karume Market in Dar es Salaam, the biggest local market for used clothes and shoes. In their places of origin they have been discarded and deposited into a charity collection bin, often in the mistaken assumption that they would subsequently be redistributed free by charity organisations to needy people in disaster zones and poorer parts of the world. In fact, the donated clothes and shoes go to sorting centres in places like Eastern Europe or Morocco, where they are separated from the unsellable clothes and prepared for resale in poorer world regions.

Secondly, the production of shoes is a global process in its own right. A shoe marked as 'Made in Italy', for instance, is Italian only in terms of its design and brand name. The leather it is made of may come from Brazil, may have been fashioned in a factory in Eastern Europe, and flown to Asia where it was sewn into a shoe that was ultimately put on the shelves of a shop in Switzerland.

As he reaches out for a second-hand shoe in Karume Market, therefore, the street vendor becomes an actor in a complex history of worldwide entanglements. As the short excerpt from an interview above shows, the vendor speaking is well aware of the global connections of his commodity and he knows how to make use of these connections to effect a sale, when he advertises a shoe 'Made in China' as a European original. Through his analytic examination of the shoes that – from his vantage point – come from remote world regions and

Street vendors find well-funded customers in the city centre, with its banks and offices.

particular pair of used shoes in Karume Market, he is displaying skills that are indispensable in this profession, if he is going to make a living from old shoes.

In Dar es Salaam, a metropolis on the shores of the Indian Ocean which is inhabited by 4.5 million people, street vendors are neither a rare nor a new phenomenon. Since it was founded in the late 19th century, the city has constantly attracted people from rural areas who wanted to escape from poverty in their villages to start a new, better life in the city. To the German and, later, British colonial administrators, however, the many young men in the streets of the city were nothing but a nuisance. The Europeans, who did not understand their ways of life and of doing business, persecuted street vendors as 'undesirables' and tried to ban them from the city.[3] After Tanganyika gained its independence in 1961,[4] many street vendors remained vulnerable to persecution and vilification by city administrators and some elements of the public. As actors in the informal economy, they do not fit the modernist vision of Dar es Salaam that some in the Tanzanian elite appear to subscribe to.[5] People working in self-organised ways in the city's backyards, sweatshops and streets constitute the informal sector that many policy makers seem to view as a kind of uncontrollable growth in the interstices of the formal

through his involvement with the respective fashions and demands of different groups of customers, he has developed a highly-specialised knowledge about the market of the streets and its dynamics. As he chooses a system. In many reports from international organisations, such as the International Labour Organization (ILO), self-organised ways of trading that circumvent official regulations are labelled as 'informal'.[6] This word characterises such ways of doing business mostly in terms of what it is not, does not have, or is unable of doing. The informal economy is typified by a lack of appropriate business permits, violation of zoning codes, failure to report tax liabilities, noncompliance with labour regulations, use of illegal means to produce legal products, and so on.[7] In other words, the notion of an informal economy is built on the idea that there is a *proper* way of doing business that *correctly* follows official regulations, and that this is in contrast to a *deviant* form of business. The notion of informal economy thus also entails a cultural valuation of what is *regular* and what is supposed to be *irregular* and, therefore, *illicit*. This concept is, however, unsuitable for an anthropological approach to street vending.

An anthropological approach to street vending aims to understand the cultural and social forms which actors give to their everyday life and work from their own point of view, instead of juxtaposing it with an official account of how business is supposed to be organised, according to sanctioned regulations. Once the negative definition of street vending as an informal economy is put aside, the skills and specialised knowledge that are constitutive of this form of practice come to the fore. For that reason, the shoe vendors introduced in this book are understood as experts who have jointly created an impressive volume of knowledge about the city and its inhabitants. While this knowledge is based on individual street vendors' experiences in the streets, it is constantly shared and updated in interactions and conversations with colleagues and peers. In this way, the shoe vendors together produce an understanding of the city as a market. It is important to add that this market is not a physical space which is clearly demarcated and set apart from wider social life in the city, such as a marketplace that people only enter if they want to buy or sell something. In fact, the people in the city who the street vendors try to sell to may have other things on their minds whilst walking along the streets, rather than buying a pair of shoes. The sellers' biggest challenge therefore is to create a market where none exists, one that lasts just for the length of a conversation, as an interruption to potential customers' other everyday activities.

The exhibition and the book *Making a living from old shoes: Tanzanian street vendors as urban experts* therefore does not primarily discuss objects or a museum collection, but the everyday practices of a group of shoe vendors. The scientific basis for this is the 15 months of ethnographic fieldwork that I conducted with a group of around 45 shoe vendors in Dar es Salaam between 2011 and 2013. This book only focuses on one group of male street vendors, although many women in Dar es Salaam also support themselves and their families through self-generated economic activities.[8] While men in the city often work without any European type of employment contract, as construction workers and craftsmen, in transport or as vendors of electronic equipment, housewares or clothes, women often prepare and sell foodstuffs and meals in their homes, street stalls or cafés in the city. The different possibilities, prospects and life worlds of men and women in Dar es Salaam would undoubtedly make an interesting study in its own right. However, during my research, I mostly came into contact with male street vendors – certainly due to my own gender – so the focus of this book is limited to male workers in what is labelled the informal sector.

Anthropological fieldwork is characterised by the particular quality of its results. These results are generally not gathered from standardised questionnaires or by analysing statistical data, but from personal experiences gained in myriad encounters, conversations and shared practices with people in specific social contexts.

Anthropology is not merely about revealing the complex relationships that make up social and cultural life, but understanding from the subjects' own point of view how they make *sense* and give *meaning* to these relationships in their everyday life. Reaching that level of understanding requires a lot of time and – above all – respectful and trusting relations between the researcher and the people that she or he wishes to study. In order to understand how people give meaning to their own place in the world, it is vital to learn their language. Since anthropological research is about people's everyday practices, there is only one way to fully understand these practices: through the fieldworker's direct participation. Only participant observation, the main method of anthropological research, allows us to understand those aspects of cultural knowledge that are rarely articulated by the actors themselves – or that are even impossible to convey via language. This method allows us to experience the aspects that other methods, such as interviewing, may not be able to grasp.[9]

In the exhibition *Making a living from old shoes*, visitors are given the opportunity to create their own experiences as street vendors in a similar way – to some degree at least – through the computer simulation *Sole City*.[10] In the simulation, visitors take on the role of a street vendor and thus turn into researchers gaining their own understanding of the life world of street vendors. This experience allows them to understand the challenges that street vendors face every day in a much more immersive and realistic way than purely audiovisual or textual media in an exhibition would. *Sole City* conveys a feeling of the pressures that street vendors are subjected to every day: the need to make the right decisions within seconds, the insecurity of being persecuted by the police for engaging in an illicit business, the frustration of spending days out in the streets without earning enough money to provide for the family back home. By participating in *Sole City*, visitors not only learn about the life worlds of street vendors in an African city, but simultaneously learn something about the process of knowledge production in anthropological research. In that respect, the simulation is a pilot project for the Ethnographic Museum at the University of Zurich, since *Sole City* allows us to explore the possibilities that participative media might provide to inform our visitors about a particular exhibition's subject, but also about the methodological approach used in anthropological research more generally.

In this book, the ethnography on shoe vendors in Dar es Salaam is supplemented by two contributions about the journeys which the shoes themselves take around the world. In her chapter, Tabea Grob argues for more transparency about the global trade in second-hand clothes and shoes, which benefits from donors' mistaken belief that their clothes and shoes will be given directly to needy people as an act of charity. In reality, however, the over-consumption of clothes and shoes in the rich parts of the world produces a surplus in second-hand clothes that would overstretch charity organisations' capacities to collect, sort and transport them. For that reason, commercial companies today collect used clothes and shoes, singling out unsellable items and recycling them, whilst trading sellable clothes and shoes to intermediary profit-making dealers, who then distribute them worldwide. Some of their profits go to charitable organisations. The huge amounts of second-hand clothes and shoes that reach local markets all over the world at low prices are both a boon and a bane for local consumers. On the one hand, second-hand clothes are in high demand due to their relative good quality. On the other hand, however, local textile and shoe producers cannot compete with these cheap imports.[11] In Tanzania, for example, many thousands of jobs have been lost in the textile industries since the recent increase in second-hand imports.

As Christa Luginbühl's chapter shows, even the shoe production process itself raises some sociopolitical issues. Shoe producers today outsource labour-intensive steps to foreign countries where wages are lower and employees' rights are often ignored in order to maximise profits. The workers in these countries do not benefit at all from the larger profit margins, however. In tanneries and sewing plants, people work in precarious conditions to facilitate the over-consumption of purchasers in the wealthier parts of the world. In fact, it seems to be just as difficult to make a living producing new shoes in Europe as it is by selling old shoes in Tanzania.

Acknowledgements

Christa Luginbühl's contribution on the global shoe industry's production processes, and Tabea Grob's chapter on clothing donations in Switzerland and the worldwide trade in second-hand clothes both complement my research on street vending in Tanzania. I thank Christa Luginbühl and Tabea Grob for their valuable cooperation.

Long before I started to think about the best way to present the results of my research in a museum exhi-

bition, I planned my fieldwork in an office at the University of Constance, where I worked as an assistant to Thomas G. Kirsch, who was also my doctorate supervisor. I am grateful to Thomas Kirsch for his support.

My fieldwork in Dar es Salaam was financially supported by the German Academic Exchange Service (DAAD)'s 'PROMOS' programme and by the University of Constance's Cluster of Excellence: 'Cultural Foundations of Social Integration'. I thank the DAAD and the Cluster of Excellence for their kind support.

My entrance to the field was facilitated by a research permit granted by the Tanzania Commission for Science and Technology (COSTECH). I am grateful to the staff of COSTECH for their trust in me.

Colman Titus Msoka of the University of Dar es Salaam supported my application for research clearance, and I would like to thank him for his help.

The computer game *Sole City* was created through international and interdisciplinary cooperation between the Ethnographic Museum at the University of Zurich, the Tanzanian photographer Link Reuben and the Austrian artist collective gold extra.[12] I thank the team of gold extra for their creative assistance on my project. I am also grateful to Link Reuben for his photographs and videos, which not only provided the basis for the graphic design of *Sole City*, but were also shown in the exhibition and enrich this book.

I am grateful to the Ernst Göhner Foundation and the Swiss National Science Foundation (SNF), which both financially supported the production of *Sole City*.

It is a special privilege to have the opportunity to share the results of my fieldwork in a museum exhibition. I thank the entire team of the Ethnographic Museum, under the supervision of Mareile Flitsch.

My special thanks go to the shoe vendors and their families in Dar es Salaam and their rural home village, Miungo. They welcomed me and allowed me to learn from them.

1 Excerpt from an interview with Chedo, June 11, 2011.
2 Appadurai 1997.
3 Burton 2007.
4 The mainland part of Tanzania, Tanganyika, gained independence in 1961 and in 1964 united with Zanzibar to form the United Republic of Tanzania.
5 Lyons et al. 2012: 1016f., 1024f.
6 Hart 1973; International Labour Organization 2013a; International Labour Organization 2013b.
7 Brown et al. 2010: 667.
8 Msoka 2005.
9 Dewalt and Dewalt 2011; Bernard 2011.
10 *Sole City* can be downloaded at www.musethno.uzh.ch/solecity.
11 Frazer 2008.
12 www.link-reuben.com; www.goldextra.com.

Karume Market is the largest outlet for second-hand shoes in Dar es Salaam.

Alexis Malefakis

The second-hand market in Dar es Salaam

Tanzania is one of the most important outlets for second-hand clothes and shoes in the world. An entire profession has developed that deals in second-hand clothes. In Dar es Salaam, it is mainly rural migrants who make a living from selling used clothes and shoes in the streets.

In 2014, Tanzania imported around 116,000 tonnes of second-hand clothes, 40,000 of which came from Asia, 36,000 tonnes from the USA and 12,000 tonnes from Europe.[1] Tanzania is the seventh largest importer of second-hand clothes in the world. On the African continent, only Mozambique imports more second-hand clothes than Tanzania. In some African countries, however, such as Nigeria, Zimbabwe and Ethiopia, it is illegal to import used clothes and shoes, due to hygienic considerations and concerns that second-hand clothes may pose health hazards to consumers. In addition, some of these countries argue that these cheap second-hand imports would bring local producers to their knees – a fear that has proven true for Tanzania.

During the 1960s and 1970s, Tanzania's local textile industries were able to satisfy domestic demand for materials and garments.[2] Even though second-hand clothes were available in Tanzania during this era, they were either smuggled goods or distributed to the population by church missions. The importation of second-hand clothes was officially prohibited, in accordance with the socialist political philosophy of the first president of the United Republic of Tanzania, Julius Kambarage Nyerere (*1922; †1999). Through a political programme of self-reliance, he propagated the all-encompassing self-determination and socioeconomic autarky of Tanzanians from its former colonial rulers and the West in general. According to his vision, it was unthinkable that free and independent Tanzanians would choose to dress themselves in the discarded attire of their former colonial oppressors.[3] However, during the 1980s and 1990s, several factors led to an increase in imports of second-hand clothes and other used commodities into Tanzania. One reason was a shortfall in local supplies of cotton. Frequent electricity cuts rendered continuous production in industries all over the country impossible and, thus, diminished their chances for survival.[4] Most importantly, however, in the late 1980s and 1990s the World Bank and International Monetary Fund (IMF) imposed structural adjustment measures[5] which negatively affected the situation of local producers dramatically. During the 1970s, the Tanzanian economy had already deteriorated due to a global economic crisis that resulted in a sharp fall in prices for the country's agricultural products on the world market. Two droughts in 1974 and 1979 decimated agricultural production, and the war with Uganda in 1978 worsened the economic situation still further. In 1979, Tanzania had to start negotiations with the IMF in order to obtain financial support and, in 1986, agreed to implement a series of structural adjustments to its economy as a condition for obtaining credits from the international donor community.[6] This included reducing government expenditure considerably, which led to cutbacks in social services and redundancies for those employed in state organisations.[7] In accordance with the IMF requirements, the public sector had to be privatised and downsized, which led to a further increase in unemployment. The donor community required Tanzania to abandon the African socialist political system implemented by the state's founder Nyerere, and replace it with a capitalist economic system. Financial investments were made, especially in the commercial sector, but little money was invested into manufacturing industries. In those years, the volume, but also the range of used goods (cars, furniture, clothes and shoes) imported into Tanzania increased considerably.[8]

The era of the World Bank and the IMF structural adjustment programmes marks the beginning of the 'success story' of *mitumba*, as second-hand clothes and other used goods are called in Swahili. Local textile producers, however, could not compete with the dramatic increase in second-hand clothes which became available at local markets all over the country. It is difficult to estimate the precise number of jobs that were lost in the Tanzanian textile industry from the 1990s on, as many

employees in small and medium-sized companies were not recorded in official statistics, but it was certainly a few thousand at least.[9] It is possible that people who lost their jobs in the manufacturing industries are now

23

Dar es Salaam has always been a commercial city. The market area of Kariakoo is its economic heart.

earning their livelihoods by importing and trading second-hand clothes, but no research has yet been conducted into this question.

Many cities in Africa have grown rapidly over the last few decades. The population of Dar es Salaam, for instance, has increased almost a thousandfold since it was founded in the 1880s. In 1886 there were around 5,000 people living in a small settlement on the harbour bay, whereas today there is a population of 4.5 million people.[10] Ever since its early days, the city has always been a magnet for people from rural areas seeking to escape the harsh living conditions and poverty of their villages and build a better life in the city. However, most of these newcomers do not find jobs that would fit a European notion of regular work: one with an employment contract, social security arrangements, holiday and sick pay entitlements and a regular salary. In fact, such conditions of employment are the exception for the majority of Dar es Salaam's working population. Most of the thousands of rural migrants who arrive in the city every year are unable to secure work in the formal sector comprised of banks, offices, ministries, companies and shops. Therefore, many people are forced to generate their own economic activities, to eke out a subsistence by themselves. To do this, they cooperate closely

with their neighbours and peers, their relatives and acquaintances from their home regions, in order to gain access to capital, commodities, tools and markets. The notion of *networking* that is so widespread among urban professionals in Europe is of existential significance for the people in Dar es Salaam. Because so few people have employment security and as there is no health and welfare system to support the unemployed, most of Dar es Salaam's inhabitants are completely dependent on their personal networks of cooperation for survival.

In this respect, the trade in second-hand clothes for many people is also a precarious business. A large proportion of the second-hand clothes and shoes imported to Tanzania are not resold through licensed shops, but through the individual street vendors who walk the streets of cities such as Dar es Salaam. Lacking employment status or rights, they have to create their own access to goods and markets. Instead of contractual regulations, the most important factors for organising this are kinship and neighbourhood relations or membership of a particular ethnic group.

To describe this mode of urban social organisation, the sociologist and urban researcher AbdouMaliq Simone coined the term 'people as infrastructure'.[11] In common parlance, infrastructure denotes the material networks and systems that organise and reproduce social life. Streets, wires and cables connect people and give them access to centrally-provided resources and services. The notion of people as infrastructure, on the other hand, stresses the significance of the activities undertaken by individuals themselves, and the ways that they establish complex formations of objects, spaces, people and practices which allow them to run their daily lives.

Visiting Dar es Salaam as a West European, one immediately notices how the material infrastructure of the city seems to be exhausted, in contrast to the city's vibrant social life. The narrow roads leading from the harbour and the city centre out to the north, west and south of the city are hopelessly overburdened with the mass of goods and people, as traffic rolls into the hinterlands of Tanzania and beyond. Private cars and *daladala* minibuses transporting commuters from residential areas to the city centre are stuck in extensive traffic jams that span the entire city each day. Connecting streets between the main arterial roads are mostly unsurfaced. Residential areas only have dirt roads and trails, which turn into mud and swamps during the rainy season.

The city's electricity grid is outdated and overloaded, and the amount of electricity it stores and supplies cannot meet the city's growing demands. In fact, electricity is so scarce in Dar es Salaam that its use is rationed most days, with some parts of the city lacking electricity for up to ten hours per day. This makes it impossible for small and medium-sized enterprises to operate reliably, and the busy city centre is dominated by the sound of generators whirring away in streets and backyards. Fresh drinking water is only sometimes available through the obsolete water supply network. Private households, which are often not connected to the main water system, obtain water from local wells, which frequently proves impossible because they cannot run their electric water pumps. Households that do not have access to local wells are forced to buy water in plastic canisters from private water vendors. Meanwhile, only about 10 percent of households are connected to the waste water system that was built in the 1980s and is, today, in "various stages of disrepair".[12] All of this clearly shows that the city's material infrastructure was not constructed for the millions of people living there today, and is therefore unable to support them.

Yet, despite everything, Dar es Salaam is a 'functioning' city that pulses with a vibrant interplay of mundane activities, even in the smallest of spaces: cooking, eating, selling, buying, loading, unloading, bartering, fighting, relaxing, greeting, laughing.[13] It is true that the infrastructural deficiencies might be a nuisance for European visitors in Dar es Salaam. But the city's inhabitants were not attracted to the city by the promise of an easy life. People who leave their villages to move to the city often do so because they are seeking opportunities to earn income, which is absent from their rural homes. Many people in rural areas subsist on the yields of their fields and their livestock farming, which is often scarcely enough to get by on. They are only able to obtain any cash at all if they manage to generate small farming surpluses to sell at local or regional markets. Therefore, rural life offers little prospect, especially for young people who may dream of a life with a nominal amount of personal and financial security. In contrast, the city appears to offer a promising alternative. The unabated influx of people from villages into Dar es Salaam attests to this perception and means that demographic pressure on the city will continue to grow immensely. It is expected that up to 200,000 people will migrate to Dar es Salaam every year.[14] According to an estimate by the African Development Bank, more than 20 million people will live in the city by 2052.[15]

In Dar es Salaam, self-generated work is not a marginal phenomenon, but a commonplace way of life. An official survey from 2000 found that more than 60

percent of households in Dar es Salaam partly or entirely rely on income generated in the informal sector.[16] The city's population has nearly doubled since then, and the importance of self-generated economic activities has not declined. More than 700,000 such traders on the city's streets attest to the significance of this sort of work for the urban economy.[17]

A brief history of urbanisation and street vending in Dar es Salaam

In the days when Dar es Salaam was being developed into a capital city by first the German and, later, British colonial rulers, rural immigrants who tried to make a living for themselves in the city were considered to be "undesirables".[18] The city's colonial masterplan reserved the central business district for Europeans and Asians, and Africans who were caught there without a satisfactory reason for their presence risked being arrested, re-

Water, clothes, snacks or toothpaste: street vendors have perfected the art of distributing goods to meet their customers' demands. But anyone working without an official permit runs the risk of prosecution.

moved from the city and repatriated to the countryside. But, because living conditions in rural areas were so harsh, people tended to return to the city after a short time.

The per head taxation introduced by the colonial administration forced people to work on the foreigners' commercial plantations in order to earn the money they needed to pay their taxes.[19] From the rural perspective, moving to the city was associated with the hope of making a life with more self-determination and dignity. Even in colonial times, rural migrants created some income opportunities for themselves by making and selling meals and other items of daily life in the streets and residential areas. However, the British colonial government incessantly tried to restrict Africans' movement into the city. They believed that the many young people walking along the streets selling foodstuffs and household supplies posed a constant nuisance since, as self-organised workers, they eluded colonial control completely. Because the authorities did not understand these people's ways of living and working,[20] they considered them petty criminals or scroungers and a general threat to public order.[21]

The condescending attitude which the colonial administrators had towards the urban population's ways of doing business apparently left its mark on the postcolonial elite's vision of the city. Tanganyika's independence from British rule in 1961 brought some fundamental changes for rural and urban populations alike. Yet, even though the un- and underemployed young people of Dar es Salaam had supported Julius Nyerere's Tanganyika African National Union (TANU) in force from the 1950s on, his administration continued to criminalise and evict from the city those inhabitants who earned their livelihoods in self-organised ways, so still counted as unemployed in official statistics.[22]

Even today, the Tanzanian government retains a largely negative attitude towards the thousands of young people who try to make a living in the streets. Street vendors and other workers who lack official registrations and licences live and work with the constant threat of raids, confiscations and imprisonment. On the one hand, it has often been argued that the informal sector has contributed significantly to the country's gross domestic product since the era of structural adjustment in the 1980s and 1990s, and therefore ought to be considered a growth factor in its own right.[23] But, on the other hand, official policy still aims to register and licence all small-scale businesses in order to bring them under state control.[24] Without such licences, small-scale entrepreneurs remain exposed to the constant threat of persecution. While it is true that stationary small businesses can now register their kiosk or market stall, some of the registration regulations exclude mobile street vendors from the outset. The need to provide a permanent business address, for example, or to display the registration form visibly on a wall inside the business premises, makes the process completely unfeasible for mobile street vendors.[25]

1   UN Comtrade Database.
2   Kinabo 2004.
3   Rivoli 2005: 190.
4   Kinabo 2004.
5   Structural adjustment programmes are the economic and political measures which the IMF and the World Bank impose as a condition for allocating credits to countries in the Global South. These programmes are tailored to the specific situation of the respective countries, but generally aim to privatise public-sector enterprises and to deregulate domestic markets.
6   Costello 1996: 139.
7   Lugalla 1997.
8   Msoka 2005: 53.
9   Hütz-Adams 1995.
10 National Bureau of Statistics Tanzania et al. 2013.
11 Simone 2004.
12 World Bank 2012: 5.
13 cf. Simone 2004.
14 United Nations Human Settlements Programme 2014: 149.
15 Sturgis 2015.
16 National Bureau of Statistics Tanzania 2002.
17 Lyons and Msoka 2010: 1082.
18 Brennan and Burton 2007; Burton 2005; Burton 2006; Burton 2007; Mbilinyi 1985; Leslie 1963; Iliffe 1979.
19 Lugalla 1997: 42; Mbilinyi 1985: 90.
20 Iliffe 1979: 36.
21 Leslie 1963; Mbilinyi 1985: 89.
22 Burton 2007: 140.
23 Luvanga 1996: 2.
24 Lyons et al. 2012.
25 Ibid: 1023.

Alexis Malefakis

An anthropological approach to street vendors' skills

Ethnographic research is based on direct participation and personal conversations with the people whose lives and work is being studied. All cultural practices entail forms of experiential knowledge that may be difficult or even impossible to verbalise, but may be understood through direct experience. The complex relationship between experience, knowledge, practice and language can be understood by analysing the work routines of shoe vendors in Dar es Salaam.

Many economic and social scientific studies discuss self-organised forms of work and business in terms of an informal economy. From an anthropological standpoint, however, the distinction between the formal and the informal is of little analytical value, because the concept of formal or informal rests on normative definitions of which types of economic activity should be considered 'proper' or 'illicit' and, therefore, illegal. For an anthropological account of street vending, however, it is little use to state that such kinds of self-generated economic activities do not comply with state regulations. Instead, through dialogue and by participating in their daily practices, an anthropological approach aims to understand how street vendors organise their life and work routines, and which complex cultural and social forms they create through these practices.

Such an anthropological analysis of self-organised work routines offers insights into the more general processes which enable people to create structures in the form of knowledge and established practice through their daily activities. This, in turn, reveals how these forms of knowledge and practice have a structuring effect on their subsequent actions and practices.[1] In order to achieve this, however, it is necessary for the anthropological approach to free its analytical gaze from the potential biases caused by cultural concepts and notions from the anthropologist's own culture. The aim of an ethnographic account is to recount and analyse the lifeworld of people under study from their own perspective, rather than from the viewpoint of an outsider or mere onlooker. One suitable method to gain this emic point of view is participant observation of their mundane activities. Instead of preparing questionnaires with standardised questions or interpreting statistical data, the ethnologist enters the field of study themself, learns the local language, shares their time and history with the people whose life they are interested in, participates in their social life and, thus, learns to understand their subjects' lifeworld on their own terms.

Between 2011 and 2013 I lived in Dar es Salaam for a total of 15 months. During that time, I studied the everyday work routines of a group of about 45 male shoe vendors through the methods of participant observation, ethnographic interviews and informal conversation. Almost all of the shoe vendors I worked with were Wayao (singular Mwyao), members of the ethnic and language group Yao, which is mainly indigenous to Malawi but also in the north of Mozambique and the south of Tanzania. The Wayao I worked with all came from the same village in the southern region of Mtwara and were related to one another through kinship ties. Most of them were between 25 and 35 years old. The relative homogeneity of the group in terms of ethnicity and kinship was caused by the pattern of rural-urban migration among the Wayao. As they explained to me, it was a common course of action for the young men to leave their village on completion of seven years' primary school education and stay with a relative in Dar es Salaam in the hope of finding better life chances there. During their first months in the city, they lived with their hosts, until they were urged to find their own means of income. In most cases, it made sense for the new migrant to follow his host into the line of business in which he had already established himself over several years. For a young Mwyao moving in with an older relative in Dar es Salaam who was a mobile shoe vendor, this therefore meant that he would soon become a street vendor on the city streets himself.

If the host had earned enough money the previous day to buy some new merchandise, he would take his young relative with him to Karume Market, the largest market selling second-hand clothes and shoes in the bustling Kariakoo market area in the heart of the city. There he would show his apprentice how to choose certain pairs out of the large heaps of shoes that would appeal to the specific group of customers he focused on. This practice of se-

There is not much for young people in the shoe vendors' rural homestead, except for hard work and poverty.

lecting the right shoes was called *kupoint* by the shoe vendors, and this ostensibly trivial practice entailed complex forms of experience and knowledge which the traders had gathered and perfected over many years of practice. *Kupoint* had far-reaching consequences for a vendor's working day, because the kinds of shoes he

35

chose in the early morning hours in Karume Market determined what kinds of customers he would attract later on in the streets. The different kinds of customers were known to have very different buying behaviours and spending capacities.

Next, he would take his young relative to his colleagues in a small backyard in the inner city, where the shoe vendors had established their *kijiweni*[2] – their meeting point and workshop. He showed him how to wash the dust off the second-hand shoes with some water and washing powder, how to repair scuffed rubber soles and shine them with shoe polish. The few tools that he needed for this were shared among groups of colleagues at the *kijiweni*. They bought brushes, shoe polish, razor blades, rubber soles and superglue for a few hundred shillings from a small kiosk in Karume Market that catered to the special needs of the shoe vendors who went there to look for sellable items. Then he would take him out into the streets to teach him how to spot potential customers, how to talk to them, how to negotiate prices and, ultimately, how to sell them a pair of shoes. After a couple of days, he would give him a few of his own pairs of shoes to gain some experience himself. If he was successful, he would give him a share of his profits, to enable the apprentice to build up his own capital over a few more days. This would even-

tually allow him to go to Karume Market on his own account, to rummage through the piles of shoes, look for suitable items and, thus, start his own business.

My fieldwork with the shoe vendors started at their *kijiweni*. It took a couple of weeks before I established friendly contact with some of them and became accepted as an exotic yet harmless alien amongst them. Whenever I got the chance, I introduced myself and explained – as well as I could in my then very basic Swahili – my intention to learn more about their work as part of my research into street trading. Initially, the shoe vendors were unfamiliar with the concept of anthropological field research, but most of them welcomed me and were happy that I was interested in their work and life. I had countless conversations with all of them over the following months, interviewed many in different situations about diverse aspects of their work, accompanied them to Karume Market, on their journeys through the streets to their homes in an urban residential area and, also, to their home village in the south of the country.

After a few more weeks, I started to buy my own pairs of shoes in Karume Market, repaired and polished them at the *kijiweni* and started selling them on the pavement in front of the backyard, where the shoe vendors also started their business day, before taking to the streets.

37

My first clumsy attempts to talk to customers and
discuss styles and prices with them doubtlessly contributed to the entertainment of the entire group of shoe
vendors at the *kijiweni*. Although I found these experiences
challenging, they certainly signalled to my new shoe
vending colleagues that I meant business when I wanted to learn as much as possible about selling shoes
in the streets. In terms of ethnographic research, this participant observation allowed me to understand those
aspects of their cultural practice that were difficult, if not
impossible, to explain in conversations and interviews.
The specific forms of attentiveness in the streets, the corporeal tensions one experiences when police officers
appear around the corner, or the profound exhaustion after
a day in the streets when one has blisters on one's
feet without having earned a single shilling – these dimensions of experience cannot simply be retrieved in
interviews.[3] In this way, I learned that the things the shoe
vendors needed to know and do in order to be successful in their business were much more complex than
could be described in a conversation.

The urban expertise of street vendors

Specialised knowledge is the basis of the street vendors'
success. They have to understand which styles of shoes are
in fashion on the streets of Dar es Salaam at the moment; which different kinds of customers there are and what
particular tastes in shoes they have; where they are
most likely to encounter the various kinds of customers at
which times of the day; how best to approach the different groups of customers; and what level of prices they
are prepared to pay for which types of shoes. This knowledge, however, was not gained from theorising about the
market of the streets, but through their practical engagement with social life in the streets of the city. Only by
actively engaging with people in the streets did they
learn how to behave, act and react. With each new successful or unsuccessful sales pitch, they learned about new
characteristics of particular kinds of customer and, by sharing these individual experiences with their peers, they
established elaborate classifications of customers, shoes,
types of encounters and sales tactics. These classifications were solidified into slang expressions, such as the
term *kupiga fos*, a particular sales tactic, or *viatu vya
kibibi*, a specific kind of shoe that can be sold to a particular
kind of customer in a particular way.

The experience and knowledge entailed in these verbal expressions, however, are not purely linguistic in nature. The knowledge of street vendors does not merely comprise 'information' about the market that can be shared verbally. It is an anthropological understanding that people know many more things, and some completely different things than they are able to express in their respective language. Yet language is not only an important medium for communication, but it also structures our understanding of the world we live in, in significant ways. Linguists have argued that the grammar of a language determines the ways in which a speaker of that language conceives of the world and makes sense of it.[4] According to this idea, language structures our thinking. Just like words in a sentence, one thought follows another in a logical sequence. However, this notion that thinking and knowledge are sentence-like and sequential does not help us decipher, for instance, the complex operations of an artisan at work.[5] If we want to understand an artisan's skills, it is not enough to base our analysis on what they can tell us they know in an interview. The true skill of an artisan lies in the complex interplay of their body, and the material and tools they use.[6] In fact, this is true for all human activities – ploughing a field, operating a machine or even,

simply, walking involves culturally-constructed corporeal forms of knowledge.[7]

The anthropologist Maurice Bloch suggested that knowledge should not be understood as being constructed in the same way as language, but as resembling network-like structures instead.[8] He argues that the

Fancy shoes for 'fashionable girls': the shoe vendors can make a good profit if they can match the taste of well-off customers.

concepts which we use to give order to the world around us and which help us to organise our practices are not structured as individual propositions that logically follow one another, like words in a sentence. For example, in order to be able to recognise a 'house', we do not have to process a checklist, such as whether or not there is a door, a window, a roof, and so on. Rather, we are able to recognise within a fraction of a second whether we are opposite a house or not.[9] Furthermore, Bloch argues that the different characteristics of a 'house', are not listed in our thinking, but are tightly packed inside a network that allows us to match the perceived reality with our knowledge about it. If, on the other hand, thinking was a linear process in which reality was checked along a single line of thought and decisions made in the same sequential way, he says, we would not be able to explain the efficiency and sheer speed with which humans think and act.

I quickly understood the significance of this concept of knowledge as an interplay of cognitive and practical concepts when I learned how to move through the streets of Dar es Salaam like a shoe vendor. A street trader has to assess within seconds whether a passer-by is a potential customer or not, has to quickly evaluate their possible taste and spending power, and react swiftly using the most appropriate sales pitch. In order to transform random encounters in the streets into sales opportunities, a street seller needs to have the skills to make the right decisions as quick as a wink. The shoe vendors, for example, had to classify passing pedestrians according to the customer categories they had established over the course of many years in the business. Then they had to choose a pair of shoes from those in their hands that were likely not only to match her taste, but also to fit her feet. With the right shoes in hand, they had to attract her attention, because the vendors told me that, once she had walked past, her mind was already occupied with completely different things and the chance to sell her something was lost.

The practice of street selling revealed structuring moments, since it generated forms of knowledge that were invoked in practice and which, in turn, had a structuring effect on the emergent practice.[10] The shoe vendors' knowledge was based on their practical engagement with their environment, with the shoes in their hands, the tools they used, the social spaces of the city, the architecture of the streets, the passers-by and police officers they encountered, and – a factor not to be underestimated – with their colleagues at the *kijiweni*. Their knowledge and skills were grounded in individual experience, but became communicable by being transformed into verbal slang expressions. Through their conversations and interactions at the *kijiweni*, the shoe vendors' experiences were solidified into metaphors and nicknames for types of shoes and customers which entailed typologies and programmes for action that had previously proven to be efficient solutions to recurring situations and problems in the streets.

In the beginning, I had to admit, I hardly understood what the shoe vendors meant when they were talking about their 'poisonous' shoes or their encounters with 'fashionable girls'. My process of knowledge production in fieldwork was characterised by practical learning as well. It was only after I began visiting Karume Market in the morning and eventually started to *kupoint* the shoes I deemed sellable to different kinds of customers in the streets I appreciated the scope of the shoe vendors' knowledge strategies.

Notes from the field: A morning at Karume Market

One early morning in June I have an appointment with Chedo in front of Karume Market in the heart of Dar es Salaam. We meet at the bus stop opposite the market entrance. Today he wants to show me where he and his colleagues buy their shoes in the morning. But first we sit under a tree at the bus stand and drink *kahawa*, a kind of strong mocha typically sold in Dar es Salaam's streets. "Watch out for your money and

*Shoe polish, laces, superglue:
a kiosk in Karume Market sells the
tools that shoe vendors need.*

your phone, there are a lot of pickpockets around," Chedo advises me a little later, as we start moving into the market crowd. I reach for the phone in my front pocket and follow him.

The part of the market we enter is reserved for selling used shoes. Market vendors sell from self-built market stalls. Simple wooden platforms, about 1.5 metres square. Narrow paths in between. A ceiling of corrugated iron above them, resting on wooden beams. Below, on the wooden tables, heaps of shoes. Helter-skelter. High-heeled shoes next to trainers, sandals between wellington boots. Winter boots next to beach flip-flops. The market traders sit on little stools and watch over their business. Wads of cash in their hands. In front of them, young men bend over the heaps of shoes, barefoot themselves. They incessantly resort the heaps in order to pull out the shoes from below to the top of the pile. Neon tubes are attached to some of the wooden beams and cast a pale light on the whole scene. Some market stalls play music from large loudspeakers, *taarab*, the music of the East African coast area. Hypnotically swaying Swahili songs flavoured with Arabian melodies and some electronic effects. The loudness of the music enhances the impression of density in the market. There is

almost no room to get through in between the market stalls. Dozens of young men dig through the shoe piles. This early in the morning, there are almost only street vendors looking for sellable shoes. None of them wants to stand in the second row while one of his colleagues might find a good bargain.

The street vendors and the market traders all seem to know one another. They hurl sarcastic insults at each other: "You're still here? I thought you'd already starved to death!" They laugh out loud, give one another high fives, move on. Chedo seems to know a lot of them as well. He greets people to the left and right, jokes around, laughs gleefully. He is at home here, he is one of them. He introduces me to some of the vendors. I look into open and friendly faces. They are suprised that I speak Swahili. They ask me my name and how I am doing. This morning I hear a lot of new names and try to memorise them.

We make a stop at one of the tables and Chedo starts rummaging through the shoe pile. Soon he produces a high-heeled shoe. Narrow heels, light brown at the front and, on top of the toes, a goldish wattlework with flowers made of plastic. Chedo nods, he seems pleased, and tells me, "this shoe is *sumu*, poison". I nod, even though I do not quite understand

what is supposed to be poisonous about the shoe, and scribble the word *sumu* in my notepad. I will ask him later why he said that. He holds the shoe by its heel and stretches his arm out in front of him. He tilts his head and narrows his eyes to slits. He seems to blank out all details of the shoe and simulates a quick glance towards it. The quick glance of a customer the way she might see the shoe in the streets. Will it attract her interest? He nods decisively. Then he puts the fingers of his right hand into the front of the shoe and checks how far they will go. I ask what he is doing. "The ladies don't like it when their toes cannot fit completely into the front of a shoe," he explains. He measures it with his fingers. "These shoes are good. They are *viatu vya masista du*, shoes for fashionable girls. *Masista du*, fashionable girls like that kind of shoe." I quickly scribble down: 'fashionable girls'.

He passes the shoe to the vendor and asks how much it costs. 22,000 shillings.[11] Chedo counters with an offer of 7,000. The vendor throws the shoe back onto the pile and immediately turns his attention to another customer. Chedo shakes his head. "He knows that he has great merchandise." He charges prices that the street vendors can barely afford, if they want to make some profit. I wonder why Chedo does not try to

bargain. "Let's wait until later, then the tables will turn," he says.

We move on to the next table. I follow Chedo's example now and start checking the shoes on the pile. Their odour reminds me of a badly-aired gym locker room. How long had they been travelling around the globe packed into plastic bales? Chedo watches my hands as they run over the different items. I pull out a flat shoe, brown leather, slight heel. Chedo nods. "These are *viatu vya kibibi*, grandmotherly shoes." I nod again and make a mental note: I will have to ask Chedo later on what he means by 'grandmotherly'. I try to examine the shoe's quality the way he does. I bend its sole in order to see how firm it still is. I run my fingers around the seam at the edge of the upper material to see whether it has come apart in any place. One of the shoes is dented at the front. But I will easily repair that at the *kijiweni*, when I wash it and stuff it with wads of old plastic rags. The leather is scuffed in some parts but, with a bit of shoe polish, nobody will notice that. "What do you think, Chedo?" I ask my companion. "Just take it, or else I will take it," he replies. I pass the shoe to the vendor. He takes it, turns it over in his fingers, then says "*kuminambili*", 12,000 shillings. That seems like a high price to me. As I had understood so far, that's the sort of price that Chedo and his colleagues often sell shoes for in the streets. There would be no profit margin at that cost. Chedo advises me: "Wait a little, it will get cheaper later on."

After our first round of the market we leave and go back to the *kahawa* vendor at the bus stop opposite. It is almost eight o'clock now. The sun has come up and now burns my skin. The *daladala*, Dar es Salaam's notorious mini-buses, speed along the street separating the market from the *kahawa* stand, leaving thick clouds of dust in the air. We sit with a couple of other men on low wooden benches, drink our *kahawa*, say nothing and rest.

When we return under the roof of the market, we first go back to the stall where Chedo had spotted the goldish shoe. But we don't find it. Someone else has bought it in the meantime. We roam around the market and go on looking for sellable shoes. I notice that the soundscape of the market has changed somewhat. The general background noise and music is now interspersed with the market traders' shouts: "*Arobaini arobaini arobaini!*" and: "*Dala dala dala dala!*" Chedo explains to me that now, later in the morning, the vendors are calling out flat prices for the leftover pairs of shoes on their tables. *Arobaini*, meaning 'forty', he

goes on, does not mean 40,000 shillings, however, but 4,000. This is something a buyer has to know. And *dala* is a code for 5,000. When the market traders realise that they have already sold their best pieces, recouped their outgoings from these sales and made some profit, they no longer bother to indulge in lengthy price negotiations for each individual pair of shoes. What is left at this point is all lower quality. "You have to understand and navigate the timing of the market in order to strike an optimal balance," Chedo elucidates. "If you arrive here too early you won't be able to afford the prices the vendors charge. But if you come too late, there is only junk left. But right now, in the middle of the morning, you get good shoes at fair prices."

After some time we reach the table where I had come across the 'grandmotherly' shoe. It is still there, but now all the shoes at this table are being sold for 5,000 shillings. I snatch at the offer. "All right!" Chedo laughs. "Get yourself some business!"

During their daily journeys, shoe
vendors take breaks at strategic points
and wait for customers.

During their daily journeys, shoe
vendors take breaks at strategic points
and wait for customers.

Of grandmothers and fashionable girls

Business on Karume Market in Kariakoo starts as early as
4am. The market traders buy their merchandise from
intermediary vendors in the harbour area, who sell entire
plastic bales that contain, for example, trousers,
shirts or shoes. Prices for those bales vary depending on
the general quality of the merchandise, which is estimated according to the goods' country of origin. Used
shoes from Korea, for instance, are sold at prices
starting from 60,000 shillings per bale.[12] This is because
the merchandise inside the bale is considered to be
of low quality and a poor match to the tastes of the different customer groups in Dar es Salaam. A bale from
Germany or the UK, on the other hand, that includes good
quality brand-name shoes, costs between 230,000
and 250,000 shillings.[13] Beyond this rather crude differen-
tiation of quality by place of export, however, the
market vendors never really know the exact quality of the
individual shoes inside their bales. They always run
the risk of buying a bale of shoes they will find difficult to
sell. For that reason, it is critical for them to quickly
make as much profit as possible, once they open their bales
in Karume Market. It is therefore essential that they
sell the best-quality pairs they saw inside their bales at the
highest possible price, to make sure that they regain
the money they have invested in the bale.

For street vendors like Chedo, these early morning
hours were a crucial part of their work routine. They had to
invest the limited capital they had at their disposal in
pairs of shoes that would attract customers of the highest

possible spending power. That was a quite complex task. The shoe vendors from the *kijiweni* catered to a market in which they themselves were not customers. With their choice of merchandise, they deliberately tried to attract women from the middle class, who worked as office clerks in ministries and banks or who studied at one of the colleges in the city centre. These customers had different tastes in clothes, and a significantly larger spending capacity, than the shoe vendors themselves. The vendors were some of the poorest people in the urban population and could not afford to be fussy about choosing their clothes and shoes. However, through their daily encounters and interactions with their better-off customers in the streets, they had acquired a thorough understanding of the fashions and styles. With his knowledge of middle-class female clothing preferences, Chedo was able to assess the shoes he encountered on the tables in Karume Market according to their marketability in the city centre. Various kinds of shoes, such as sandals, trainers or boots, were ruled out from the outset. What were in demand from his customers were elegant shoes made from precious – or, at least, seemingly precious – materials. Shoes whose origin was clearly labelled were particularly attractive. Shoes 'Made in Germany' had a good reputation with the office ladies because they

were considered to be extremely durable, Chedo explained to me. Shoes 'Made in Brazil' or 'Made in Italy' were also popular, because they were considered particularly stylish. Interestingly, shoes 'Made in China' for the European market were valued as *mitumba* in Tanzania. Their detour via European consumer markets was taken to

47

guarantee their good quality. This was in contrast to products imported directly from China, such as housewares, mobile phones and clothes, which had a rather bad reputation of being cheap but poor quality.

As well as their origin and style, the shoes' condition was crucial for Chedo's decision-making. He and his colleagues at the *kijiweni* only used a few tools to repair the shoes. After they washed them, they stuffed them with bundles of plastic rags to push them back into shape while they dried. A piece of rubber sole, a razor blade and some superglue was enough to repair a scuffed sole or heel. Black or brown shoe polish and a couple of brushes was all it took to make the upper material appear as good as new. But splits or cuts in the upper material, torn-off straps, holey soles and broken heels could not be repaired at the *kijiweni*. If a shoe was too damaged, they kept their hands off them.

Simultaneously with this general assessment, the shoe vendors classified the shoes they chose from the piles according to their own system. A shoe not only had to be generally marketable, but the vendor had to be able to anticipate what kind of customer it was most likely to appeal to. This required an understanding of when and where that kind of customer would probably be found. This knowledge was based on the individual experiences the shoes vendors had gained over the course of many years in the business.

They had devised some very specific concepts from these many individual experiences, such as the aforementioned *viatu vya kibibi*, grandmotherly shoes, or *viatu vya masista du*, shoes for fashionable girls. These terms, to be sure, did not just denote a particular style of shoes. They also comprised assumptions about certain characteristics of the different groups of customers that they associated with these kinds of shoes. This included ideas about when and where would be best to encounter them, what sales tactics were most likely to succeed with them, and what profit margins the sellers could expect to achieve. As a street vendor reached for a shoe on a pile in Karume Market, he implicitly drew on this complex knowledge. This informed grasp opened up specific future perspectives for a shoe vendor. For, with the categorisation of a shoe as 'grandmotherly', came the expectation of where his journey through the streets would lead him later on during the day, at what time, in order to encounter a 'grandmother' type.

As the shoe vendors explained to me, older ladies were mostly interested in flat shoes of a reliable quality and a reasonable price. Younger ladies, on the other hand, such as students, were looking for fancy shoes with high heels, shiny materials and elaborate adornments. These different groups of customers could be found in different areas of the city at different times of the day. The shoe vendors generally met older ladies around the ministries and at *Mahakama Kuu*, the High Court, whereas the younger ladies could be found at the Institute of Finance Management or the Tanzania Public Service College at *Magogoni*, an area near the ferry at the other side of the harbour. While students often stood in front of the colleges during the midmorning breaks between classes, the older ladies who worked inside the ministries only came out of their buildings at around noon when they went looking for lunch in one of the surrounding cafés. It was best to approach the clerks of the High Court at around 4pm, at the end of their working day.

Sales pitches for each individual group of customers took on very different forms. Older ladies, the shoe vendors had learned, were rather straightforward in conversations and only ever reacted to a street vendor's offer if they were really planning to buy something. So, if a shoe vendor had a pair of good-quality shoes in her size on offer, and the customer joined in a conversation with him, it was only a matter of agreeing a price that both sides were satisfied with. The shoe vendors' ex-

perience had taught them the downside of this type of customer, however – that older ladies had no interest in expensive shoes, so there were no large profits to be made from selling 'grandmotherly shoes'. If a street trader bought a pair of these shoes for the equivalent of two euros in Karume Market, they might resell them for four or five euros.

Students, on the other hand, were known to like spending their spare time between classes trying on shoes. For the shoe vendors, this habit offered plentiful opportunities to show them their merchandise. But, in order to convince a student to buy a pair of shoes, the vendors not only had to verbosely persuade her of the stylishness of the shoe in question and flatter her with compliments, but also to persuade her friends as well, who often commented on their friend's choice of shoes. Many such sales pitches were eventually unsuccessful. Frequently, the students simply sent the shoe vendor away at the end, saying they had no money on them anyway. However, many shoe vendors were ready to accept these frustrations, because students at certain colleges had the reputation of being high-paying customers – if a vendor could persuade them to buy something. An extravagant shoe acquired in Karume Market for the equivalent

At the kijiweni the shoe
vendors joke, fight and share
their knowledge.

of four or five euros could be sold to a 'fashionable girl' for
ten euros – or even more.

The categorisations of shoes as 'grandmotherly'
or as suitable for 'fashionable girls', thus drew on a rich
wealth of experiences with different kinds of customers in the streets and, therefore, enabled the vendors
to anticipate the course of their working day while
choosing shoes in Karume Market in the morning. Being
able to predict one's future was crucial in this line
of business. For the shoe vendors, just as for most other
street vendors who work in a highly dynamic market that is not prestructured by explicit rules, being able
to plan – at least to some degree – the activities of
their working day and the likelihood of meeting one or another type of customer offers important points of
reference.

Shared experiences: a backyard as a learning location

The *kijiweni*, a small backyard in the inner city of Dar es
Salaam, was an important meeting place for the
street vendors. They not only washed and repaired their
shoes there but it was, above all, an important social

Minor damage is repaired with simple tools.

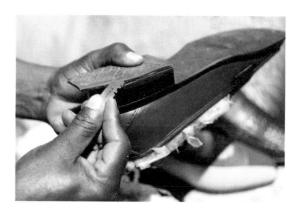

space for them. The shoe vendors shared news about colleagues and family and gossiped about friends at the *kijiweni*. Or they made arrangements to cooperate – if, for example, one of them had run out of money, they might ask one of their colleagues to give him a couple of pairs to sell for commission. Of course, the *kijiweni* was also the place where the colleagues would argue vociferously if there were any incidents of fraud or fights among them. Such quarrels could become particularly loud and passionate if they concerned the latest events in the world of football, when matches between the two local heroes *Simba* and *Yanga* or teams in the British Premier League were discussed. However, religious and moral issues that raised general issues of social life were also debated by the colleagues, such as questions of trust, fairness and respect.

While the vendors washed and repaired their new second-hand shoes, they commented on their colleagues' choice of shoes and heard their opinions about their own purchases in return. A shoe would often be passed around from one person to the next, examined and evaluated by each. Sometimes the colleagues displayed slight envy if one of them had made a particularly good bargain in Karume Market. Such a shoe would be called *sumu*, poison, indicating that a customer would quickly succumb to its appeal and pay good money for it. Such judgements might encourage a shoe vendor and bolster his self-esteem. Standing around their washing basin, exchanging their experiences in the streets and opinions about different kinds of shoes and customers, the vendors shared their knowledge about the market of the streets. Such moments provided good opportunities for me to understand how they jointly created solutions for problems which they all frequently faced in their businesses, and how they set standards for valuing shoes and customers, which provided critical reference points for each of them individually.

The vendors not only associated particular kinds of shoes with respective target customers, but they also differentiated between the types of encounters they had with passers-by on the streets. For example, Chedo and his colleagues often encountered women who liked to try shoes on and indulge in lengthy price negotiations. But, once the vendors had agreed a final price with them, they simply withdrew from the negotiations and left the scene, mumbling that they did not actually have any money on them at the moment. These kinds of passers-by, who raised the shoe vendors' expectations but ultimately just frustrated them, were called *wachawi*, witches. In this context, however, the term 'witch' did not imply any kind of belief in occult forces. A *mchawi* (singular) person was simply someone to avoid, since she would only waste their time and energy and add unnecessary frustration to a shoe vendor's working day.

It was a matter of luck, on the other hand, if they came across a *mzungu*, a white person. This *mzungu* did not necessarily have to have fair skin. The term *mzungu* in colloquial Swahili denotes a European or other person who is obviously not African. However, the shoe vendors used the word *mzungu* to denote the kind of customer who did not know how to bargain – just like many European tourists. The vendors explained that a *mzungu* would not haggle for each shilling but just pay the first price they were given. Such behaviour was unexpected from a Tanzanian, but *wazungu* (plural), that is, Europeans, were known for such incompetence in price negotiations. So, for the shoe vendors, it was a particularly lucky event if they encountered a Tanzanian *mzungu* in the streets. The odd chance of meeting a *mzungu* was also the reason why the vendors always started negotiations with extremely high – if not unreasonable – prices. This price

To get the old shoes back into shape,
they are washed and then stuffed with old
plastic rags to dry.

The vendors increase their shoes' street value by washing, repairing and polishing them.

55

was nearly always vehemently rejected by the customers. But under no circumstances did the shoe vendors want to miss the opportunity to sell a *mzungu* a pair of shoes at a ridiculously high price.

In order to determine whether a passer-by in the streets was a *mzungu*, or a *mchawi*, the vendors had developed a finely-tuned instinct for the moods and motivations of people in the streets that can hardly be put into words. Their discussions at the *kijiweni* about such issues often lasted the entire morning without ever coming to a final conclusion. The colleagues who, one by one, arrived at the *kijiweni* with their new shoes from Karume Market would join in the conversation and soon chip in with their own views and experiences. As a fieldworker, I cherished these group discussions, since they offered valuable insights into the ways that the shoe vendors perceived the city and how they made sense of its dynamism and heterogeneity. By sharing their individual experiences with their colleagues, they created a unique plane of knowledge that gave meaning to their decisions and practices. For each one of them individually, this shared meaning was a valuable form of reference.

Notes from the field: *Nyama Ngumu* – tough meat

On a Monday in February 2012, I accompany Mako on his journey along the streets. Today he has eight pairs of shoes. He carries one shoe from each pair in his hands, clutching each shoe with just a single finger – five in his right hand and three in his left. The corresponding other shoe of each pair is kept in a black plastic bag that dangles from his left wrist. Shortly before eleven o'clock, we turn into Samora Avenue. Immediately we meet a passer-by who looks at the shoes in Mako's hands. He stops, raises his hands to her eye level and addresses her: "Welcome, *anti* (aunt). I got your size here." She points at a shoe in his hand and asks: "How much for that one there?" Mako puts his shoes down on the pavement and holds the one she referred to in his hand. "Don't worry, I don't charge unreasonable prices. Why don't you just try it on first to see how it looks on your foot?" he answers. But she does not give in. "I have 7,000 shillings here. You better tell me right away whether or not you will sell it to me at this price." Mako declines. "I would go to bed hungry." He picks up his shoes and we move on.

Silently, we walk side by side for some time. Mako is not the talkative type, I have noticed that before.

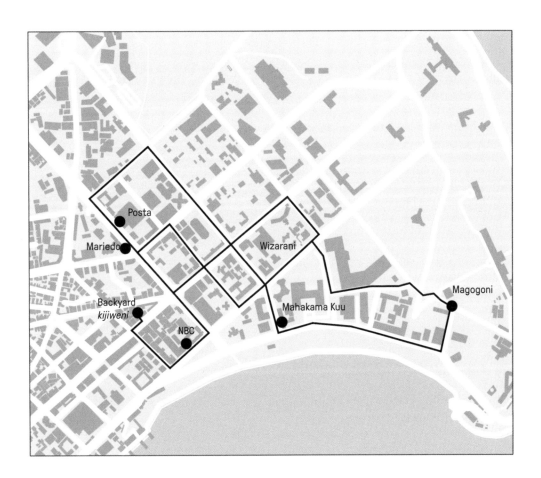

Indian Ocean

■ Map section

Dar es Salaam

Africa

Tanzania ● Dar es Salaam

Posta

Mariedo

Wizarani

Backyard
kijiweni

NBC

Mahakama Kuu

Magogoni

*The shoe vendors always walk along the same
streets on their journeys. Over the years, they have
learnt where and when to encounter certain
groups of customers.*

Instead of getting into lengthy discussions with his colleagues at the *kijiweni,* he would rather wait, listen and observe. He will only join in if something that seems relevant to him is said. Or something funny. I really like his deadpan humour. As we walk through the streets, I initially try to ask him a couple of questions. But his one-syllable answers quickly shows that he is not in the mood for conversation during his walk. So, instead of further irritating him with my questions, I now concentrate on his movements and note how he observes and assesses the passers-by we encounter. He keeps his upper body straight and holds his head up high. His arms hang down by his side, just so low that the plastic bag with the shoes in does not slide over his wrist. He walks rather quickly and I sometimes have difficulty keeping up with him as I scribble some observations in my little notepad.

As he walks, his head moves slowly from left to right in order to scan the passers-by on both sides of the street. I follow his eyes. After some time, he realises that a woman on the other side of the street has turned her head in his direction. Immediately, he crosses over to her and raises his hands with the shoes again. "*Karibu*, welcome. Just take a look at the shoes. Looking is for free," he addresses her. She touches one of the shoes and asks how much it costs. Mako puts his shoes down on the pavement. He holds the shoe in his left hand and raps on its sole with the knuckle of his right middle finger. "That is superior quality, imported from Europe. In the shops you won't get this kind of shoes for less than 60,000 shillings. But I can sell it to you much cheaper," he answers. He hands the shoe to the woman, she takes it, turns it over in her hands, examines its materials. "Really nice, how much is it?" Mako tries to stall the answer. "Just try it on first to see whether or not it fits you." But this customer does not let herself fall for this tactic. "I just want to know how much it is," she replies. "18,000," Mako answers resignedly. He seems to have already understood that there is no business to be made here. "OK", the woman says, shrugs, and hands him back the shoe. "Let's move on," Mako turns to me as he collects his shoes from the pavement.

So we walk on and scan the street for any potential customer who displays even the slightest interest in the shoes in Mako's hands. A couple of similar encounters follow, in which Mako tries to persuade his customers to try on the shoe of their liking and, thus, to bring them in further to the conversation. But none of them agrees. Their first question is always about the

price of the shoe. Mako always seems to stall by diverting the customers' attention to some detail of the shoe or its origin, quality or style. He always tries to engage the customers more physically in the conversation by putting the shoes in their hands or by trying to convince them to put them on.

Two hours later, as we continue walking in silence through the dusty streets, he suddenly turns to me and says: "You see now what it's like to walk through the streets all day without earning anything? This is *nyama ngumu!*" I write down the expression in my note-pad: *nyama ngumu* – tough meat.

It is almost one in the afternoon now. "Let's go to *Wizarani*, it's lunchtime," Mako announces as we walk on. *Wizarani*, "at the ministries" in the shoe vendors' jargon, denotes a couple of streets between the central *Posta* bus stop and the ferry port at *Kivukoni Front*. This is the area where the Ministry of Health and Social Welfare, the Ministry of Foreign Affairs, and some other government offices are located. As we arrive at the Ministry of Health and Social Welfare after ten min-utes' walk, I realise why Mako wanted to come here. Clerks are leaving their office in small groups, walking through the gate and out onto the streets. There are a lot of older ladies among them, most of them smartly

dressed. We stop at the gate and Mako puts his shoes onto the pavement, each pair neatly arranged side by side. We lean against the wall surrounding the complex. Our eyes follow the passing ladies who now head for one of the little cafés in the neighbourhood to have lunch. I am glad to rest a bit. The journeys through the streets are quite a demanding exercise for me. The blazing sun does its part. After a few minutes, Saidi joins us and arranges his shoes on the pavement right next to Mako's. After a quick exchange of greetings – we have just met a couple of hours earlier at the *kijiweni* – he turns to Mako and says: "Have you seen the empty streets today? I have not sold anything yet." "There is nothing to be gained today," Mako answers, "tough meat". Saidi agrees.

After about fifteen minutes, we take off again. "See you later at *Mariedo,*" Mako says to Saidi, as we start moving. Saidi nods, his eyes already focused on the street ahead of him.

I heard the expression *nyama ngumu*, 'tough meat', nearly every day from the shoe vendors. *Nyama ngumu* described their experience of walking along the streets for hours on end without getting the opportunity to sell a single pair of shoes. On such days, street vending was like chewing on a tough piece of meat. In theory, the meat was delicious and nutritious. But, in reality, it was so tough that you could chew it for hours without ultimately being able to swallow it and benefit from its nutrition value. In the end you would still be hungry. For the shoe vendors, this meant real hunger. If they could not sell anything, they went back home to their families empty-handed. And if they were unlucky they did not sell anything for several days in a row. 'Tough meat' was a curse for them.

The fact that the streets were often experienced as 'tough meat' was largely due to the fact that the passers-by they tried to sell to generally had other things on their minds than buying something whilst walking. They were heading to work, to lunch or to catch a bus. Buying a pair of shoes was hardly ever the reason why they were in town in the first place. In other words, for the passers-by, the streets were not a market at all. The shoe vendors, on the other hand, had to turn the streets into a market. That was their biggest challenge. They had to create selling opportunities with passers-by who were focused on other things. In order to achieve that, the vendors had developed very precise observation skills. Over the years, they had learned that there were some areas in the city where the opportunities to sell were better at certain times of the day than in other areas and at other points in time. It was nearly impossible, for example, to strike up a conversation with a passer-by at busy *Posta*. But the streets around the Ministry of Health and Social Welfare offered rather good opportunities around lunchtime. At noon, *Wizarani* was a good vending area, but not in the morning, when office clerks were hurrying through the streets on their way to their offices or were already inside their building.

In that way, the inner city was subdivided by the shoe vendors into different selling areas which all functioned according to their own temporal logic. The vendors, who preferred walking through the streets individually to avoid getting into direct competition with each other if they encountered a customer, nevertheless frequently met along the way, since they all followed a path that led them from one vending area to the next in a particular temporal sequence. Starting from *kijiweni*, they walked along a little street to NBC, the National Bank of Commerce, some hundred metres away

from their backyard. From there, they turned left to reach the bus stop at *Posta* where there was a bustle in the street at nearly all times of the day. They had a lot of encounters with passers-by, but rarely managed to turn them into selling opportunities. *Wizarani* was an important vending area on their routes, just like *Magogoni*, where the Public Service College was located. But it only made sense to go there if they had shoes for 'fashionable girls' on offer. Yet if they did, they knew that they would find the most appropriate customers at *Magogoni*.

From *Magogoni*, it was only a short walk to the High Court, *Mahakama Kuu*, located near the waterfront but on the way back to the city centre. Mako, Chedo and their colleagues liked to rest at *Mahakama Kuu* for a quarter of an hour at around 4pm, when the office clerks were leaving the building. They put their shoes on the pavement and "lay in wait" for customers, as they put it.

Around 5 or 6pm almost all of the shoe vendors went to *Mariedo*. That was a broad stretch of pavement directly outside the Benjamin Mkapa Tower, opposite the *Posta* bus stop. The name *Mariedo* was derived from a clothing store of the same name that was on the ground floor of the Mkapa Tower. However, the shop's private security guards would not tolerate any street vendors in front of the shop. So the shoe vendors' *Mariedo* had had to move up the pavement a bit and was now in front of a staircase that led to the entrance of Mkapa Tower. In the early evening hours there was a whole crowd of vendors, many colleagues from the *kijiweni* but also other street traders selling things like clothes, cigarettes and other items. The shoe vendors created one large display of their shoes, all arranging their shoes together neatly in the display. That way, we all sat and observed the incessant stream of commuters who were catching buses back to their residential areas. Whenever I went there with one of the colleagues from the *kijiweni*, I came to know new people at *Mariedo*, all street vendors from different businesses. They were often puzzled by me sitting down with them and asking them about their work. I was frequently the butt of the jokes at *Mariedo*. But my colleagues and friends from the *kijiweni* then intervened and explained that I was one of them, that I got my own shoes from Karume Market, washed them in the backyard and sold them in the streets. The others were astounded. Have things got so bad in Europe that a white man would leave his own country and come to Tanzania to learn the trade of a street vendor? The jokes slowly turned into astonished looks and, ultimately, friendly respect.

Kupiga fos – throw yourself into it! The rhythms of street vending

The shoe vendors' routes from the *kijiweni* to *Mariedo* followed a specific temporal pattern that was predetermined by the regular working hours of the employees in different offices. At the same time, however, their movements through the streets created their very own rhythms.[14] Each vending space they came to required a different kind of attentiveness and different tactics for approaching and persuading customers. At the busy *Posta*, for example, the shoe vendors had to concentrate extremely hard. There were so many people in the streets that it was generally difficult to spot potential customers. It took a high degree of attention to notice which passer-by might have shot a glance at the shoes in one's hands and thus signalled her potential readiness to buy something. Furthermore, at the crowded *Posta*, it was difficult to present oneself and one's merchandise optimally. The shoe vendors ran the risk of being overlooked if they did not actively make themselves felt. When I walked through *Posta* with one of the shoe vendors, I noticed how my body involuntarily tensed up a little and how the amount of eye contact overwhelmed my capacity to really observe and assess people.

As we moved away from *Posta*, I realised that I relaxed a little or, to be more precise, that the atmosphere changed a bit. The shoe vendors let their arms dangle at their sides and sped up their walking pace. The distance between one sales location and the next was marked by a different kind of attentiveness. We did not so much observe our immediate surroundings but, rather, scanned the street ahead of us whilst also looking for potential customers, to be ready to cross over immediately if there appeared to be a sales opportunity ahead of us.

A location such as *Mahakama Kuu*, however, required its own kind of attentiveness. Here, the shoe vendors "lay in wait" for customers, as they put it. They arranged their shoes on the pavement, backed off a little and waited until the office clerks left their building. Instead of actively approaching them the way they did while walking in the streets, they simply waited for the clerks to show an interest in a pair of shoes and approach the vendors themselves. As the shoe vendors explained, the older ladies did not appreciate being pushed or caught off-guard by street vendors. It was more advisable to give them some time to let them decide for themselves whether or not a pair of shoes appealed to them.

Therefore, if the vendors said that their tours were like 'tough meat', that did not mean that they experienced walking in the streets as monotonous. On the contrary. Their movements in the streets revealed a particular rhythm that consisted in the interplay of heightening cognitive and corporeal tensions and the subsequent release of these tensions.[15] The intense concentration in the hustle at *Posta*, for example, made way for a more general attentiveness towards passers-by at *Mahakama Kuu* or *Wizarani*. The silent miles through the streets around noon made way for the verbose moments at *Magogoni*, when the shoe vendors offered their merchandise to young students, flattering and flirting with them.

The shoe vendors knew what needed to be done if the streets were experienced as 'tough meat': they had to show complete corporeal and cognitive commitment in order to transform their random encounters into sales opportunities. The vendors displayed impressive skill in their rhetorical and psychological tactics to turn passers-by into customers. They called this skill *kupiga fos*, literally to 'use force'. In an interview, Chedo explained to me what he understood *kupiga fos* to mean in practice:

Sometimes in business you need to go crazy in order to convince a customer. You need to act as if you

*When they take a break together,
the shoe vendors arrange their shoes
into one large display.*

have lost your mind and laugh a lot. Because if she sees you laughing, she will laugh, too. And if you laugh together, that means that you have already become friends a little bit. So I tell her: "Try it on! Just try it on! Trying it on is free!" If she tries it on and sees how good it looks on her, she will ask: "How much for it?" You see? You already got her there. Then I charm her. "Is there no mirror around here? If there was a mirror, you could see just how good you look in that shoe."
Or I say, "I am an honest businessman. If a customer doesn't look good in a shoe, I don't sell it to her, but you, you look just stunning! But I wonder: is it the shoe or the foot that looks so beautiful?" Even though she can easily see through the compliment, she will laugh and say, "It's my foot, of course!" Then we laugh together. *Napiga fos!* – I throw myself into it! I tell her: "Only clever people have a taste for this merchandise. You, because you're shrewd, you have an eye for these shoes here. If you were not clever, you would not have chosen this shoe!" That's how you talk to a customer and *kupiga fos*. Because others, in the beginning, they don't even want to listen, but the longer you *kupiga fos* the more they become seduced, you convince them. In the end, she will say, "OK, let me buy something."[16]

Chedo was a real expert in *kupiga fos*. In the streets, he was particularly talkative. He laughed a lot with his customers, showered them with compliments, befriended them easily and, thus, often managed to engage them in initially non-binding and friendly conversations that he would subsequently steer in the direction of becoming a

more persuasive sales pitch. In doing so, he displayed impressive psychological skills. If the situation required it, he could become a real entertainer and stand-up comedian, thus keeping his customers' attention focused on him and his merchandise. Other shoe vendors, however, like silent Mako, were less entertaining and did not joke around with their customers. But they all knew what *kupiga fos* was all about: once they had drawn a potential customer's attention to one of their shoes, they had to do everything they could in order to keep their attention focused and engage them in a final negotiation.

Experienced shoe vendors achieved this by making use of a particular rhetorical strategy, which involved initially stalling the customer's question about how much the shoes cost. This was because, if they told them the rather high price with which they usually opened negotiations right at the beginning, customers would stop them with a wave of their hand, thank them and go on their way. In order to avoid that, the vendors usually tried to involve the customer more physically in the conversation by persuading them to try a shoe on. Once they had the shoe on their foot, their attention was entirely focused on the shoe vendor. Only then would he answer questions about the item's price.

Price negotiations usually started at a high level – 22,000, or even 25,000 shillings. As the shoe vendors told me, some customers would take it as an insult if they started at too low a price. It was more beneficial to assume that the customer was wealthy. Even if she would not pay the initial high price, she might nevertheless take it as a kind of compliment, which would create a friendly atmosphere for further negotiations. Who knew, she might even be a *mzungu* who would just pay the inflated price without bargaining.

Other than that, it was an inherent part of the conversation for the customer to decline the initial price. Instead of suggesting a lower price, the shoe vendor would ask the customer to say how much she was willing to pay. That gave him an opportunity to assess her general spending capacity. If she countered his initial price of, say, 22,000 shillings with just 3,000 shillings, he immediately knew that there was no point continuing the discussion. But, if she said 15,000, it was easy to make her add a couple of thousand shillings and thus to make a good profit. *Kupiga fos* meant not letting go of an opportunity by any means. A skilful vendor such as Chedo would use the friendly basis he had already established to tell her, for instance, that selling for 15,000 would mean that he would *kufa njaa*, starve to death. Or he would mention that his children needed new clothes and he could not afford to sell his shoes below their real value – even if he really wanted her to have the shoes, because they just looked so good on her. In this way, the conversation began in a non-committal way, but became more and more binding over the course of time.

During my first sales pitch, I made the mistake of agreeing to the price my customer offered me too early. Due to my nervousness, I simply told her that the price she had suggested was exactly the amount of money I had paid for it in Karume Market. I asked her to add some *hela ya kula*, money for something to eat, and that was it. I felt that I had made a good argument, but my shoe vending colleagues, who observed the entire show with amusement, afterwards told me that there was a major mistake in that sort of sales tactic. Once I had told the customer the price I had paid for the shoe (even if that was not the real price), she immediately knew what the lowest possible price was. All she had to do was to add 1,000 shillings, and I would be at a loss for any credible argument which would make her increase her offer. My colleagues at the *kijiweni* had plenty to laugh about that day, but I had learned some important lessons that way. Selling was all about finding out where a customer's maximum purchasing limit lay through bluffing and stating fictional prices. Selling shoes in the streets thus always involved a considerable amount of everyday psychology.

An experienced shoe vendor would, therefore, generally decline his customer's offer, knowing that she was trying to gauge where his lower limit was. Instead, he would offer her a price that was only marginally less than his initial one. If the customer did not immediately leave, he thus knew that she was really interested in the shoes and wanted to go on negotiating. Eventually, however, Chedo, Mako and their colleagues from the *kijiweni* had to accept prices that were considerably lower than their initial values. In fact, most pairs were sold at 8,000 to 12,000 shillings, equivalent to 3.50 to 5.30 euros at the time of my research. On a good day, some of them would sell three or four pairs. That way, they made enough profit to pay for a hot meal with their families at home and to go to Karume Market the next morning to buy a new couple of pairs of old shoes.

Kupiga fos was a programme for action that followed a particular script. It took great skill, however, to successfully navigate through the entire course of action, and this skill varied greatly among the shoe vendors at the *kijiweni*. Some of the younger vendors in particular, who had only been in the city for few months, found it diffi-

cult to "go crazy" in a sales pitch, as Chedo put it. During the 15 months that I spent with the shoe vendors, I got to know many youths who had to return to their village after only a few weeks of trying to sell shoes in the streets. *Kupiga fos* was not for everyone. Yet, for experienced shoe vendors, its skilful application was all their business really was about.

Kupiga fos was the central concept in the shoe vendors' work routines. When I asked them in interviews how they managed to sell shoes in the streets, they frequently referred to this concept to explain what shoe vending was all about. They also used the term in order to entice one of their colleagues, if they could see that he had not spotted a good opportunity to sell. *Nenda kapige fos!* "Go and throw yourself into it!" they shouted at him in the street, if he did not realise that a passer-by had noticed the shoes in his hands. With this exclamation, they encouraged him to strain his body and mind to focus, to run after the passer-by, to charm her and engage her in conversation and, thus, to earn a little money – instead of simply complaining about the 'tough meat' of the streets. *Kupiga fos* was a statement of pride and self-esteem for the shoe vendors, who were also wrongfully persecuted as petty criminals, despite the fact that they were honest business people.

The city as a market: street vending beyond the informal economy

The verbal symbols which the shoe vendors used to categorise different kinds of shoes, types of customers, selling areas, experiences and practices were more than merely street slang. Concepts such as 'grandmotherly shoes' or *kupiga fos* entailed complex forms of knowledge that were always linked with concrete practices and experiences. In order for me, as an anthropologist, to really understand which shoes on the piles in Karume Market should be labelled as 'grandmotherly', I had to encounter that particular group of customers in the streets and find out which behaviour they displayed in sales conversations. In order to understand the full significance of *kupiga fos*, I first had to experience how tough and frustrating the long hours walking around the streets could become. These cultural symbols comprise years of experience for many shoe vendors. The classifications and activities they denoted were important reference points which helped a street vendor to skilfully move through the city and successfully sell merchandise.

For me as an anthropologist, the street vendors' slang provided valuable insights into the ways in which they construed the city as a market. For an outsider, this market remains invisible. It is not a location in physical space, clearly marked off from wider social life in the city. The shoe vendors' market only exists in their specific understanding of the city, their inhabitants and the social dynamics of the streets. Their greatest skill is, ultimately, to jointly find access to the streets *as a market*.

Street vending as I studied it among the shoe vendors at the *kijiweni*, therefore, is anything but an arbitrary act of desperation by marginal characters. It is a profession that – just like any other profession – requires specialised knowledge and skills. Not all of them were equally endowed with the necessary skills, but those who had established themselves as successful street vendors over the years had together created cultural notions and forms of knowledge whose complexity cannot even begin to be explained by the concept of an informal economy.

The notion of an informal economy may, nevertheless, remain relevant for a thorough understanding of the lifeworlds of street vendors – but from a more political dimension. Despite the fact that the concept bears little analytic value for an anthropology of street vending, it is still a normative concept that is frequently applied by elites to control less-privileged parts of society and, thus, to secure their own position of power.[17] The more than 700,000 street vendors and many other self-organised workers in Dar es Salaam[18] thus remain prone to persecution by the authorities. During raids, their merchandise is confiscated and they run the risk of being imprisoned. In order to avert that happening, however, they can bribe the police officers with a few thousand shillings. In this way, the 'formal' system happily shares in the profits of the informal economy.

1 The question of the interplay of structure and agency is one of the fundamental questions of social theory, see for example Archer 1982; Bourdieu 1976; Bourdieu 1987; Bourdieu 2000; Giddens 1997; Giddens 1979.

2 Colloquial Swahili for meeting point. Literally "at the little stone".

3 Hirschauer 2001.

4 Whorf 1988 [1963].

5 Keller and Dixon Keller 1996; Dougherty and Keller 1982.

6 Ingold 2011: 53.

7 Flitsch 2014.

8 Bloch 1991.

9 Ibid.: 185.

10 Giddens 1997.

11 At the time of research equivalent to 10 euros.

12 At the time of research equivalent to 27 euros.

13 At the time of research equivalent to 111 euros.

14 Malefakis 2015.

15 Ingold 2007: 197.

16 Interview, June 11, 2011.

17 Newell 2012: 6; MacGaffey and Bazenguissa-Ganga 2000: 5.

18 Lyons und Msoka 2010: 1082.

Tanning leather produces poisonous waste water. Many workers in this tannery in Bangladesh die before they reach 50.

Christa Luginbühl

The true cost of cheap shoes

Shoes are a global product. Shoe companies outsource the most labour-intensive parts of production to low-wage countries, in order to cut costs. Poverty-line wages, precarious working conditions and health hazards are the order of the day for workers in the supply chain. The excessive consumption of shoes and clothes adds additional fuel to the fire.

The shoe industry is a global business. Just as in the garment industry, the various individual production steps take place in multiple different countries – with the constant aim of optimising costs. Whilst most shoe design is carried out by brands, processes such as cutting, sewing and glueing are carried out by workers in factories or at home in low-wage countries. By choosing to

According to World Footwear Yearbook 2015

Top 10 Footwear Producers (Quantity) 2014

# COUNTRY		PAIRS (MILLIONS)	WORLD SHARE
1. China		15 700	64.6%
2. India		2 065	8.5%
3. Vietnam		910	3.7%
4. Brazil		900	3.7%
5. Indonesia		724	3.0%
6. Pakistan		386	1.6%
7. Turkey		320	1.3%
8. Bangladesh		315	1.3%
9. Mexico		245	1.0%
10. Italy		197	0.8%

manufacture in these low-wage countries, then sell the end products in lucrative consumer markets, shoe companies maximise their profits.

Across the world, 24.3 billion pairs of shoes were produced in 2014 – 88% of them in Asia. Shoe production in China alone amounted to 15.7 billion pairs, or 64.6% of the total. The largest European shoe producer was Italy, which produced 197 million pairs, ranking it at number 10 on the list of the world's top production countries.[1] Approximately three-quarters of the shoes produced in Asia are exported to countries outside that continent, however. Asia is not only the main exporter of shoes, but also the main consumer: more than half (52%) of the world's shoe sales take place in Asia.

Africa plays a relatively small role on the world market, both in terms of production (3%) and consumption (8%) of new shoes. The continent's top shoe exporters are South Africa (31 million pairs per year), Tunisia (22 million), Morocco (18 million), Nigeria (15 million), and the Ivory Coast (9 million).[2] A lot of the clothes and shoes sold in many African countries are imported, and a large proportion of these are second-hand goods from Europe, Asia and the USA (see Tabea Grob's chapter).

Whereas Asia mainly produces goods for the global market, almost 90% of the shoes produced in Europe end up in stores in the same continent.[3] Italy's shoe production accounts for around half of the European total, followed by Spain (13%), Portugal (12%) and Romania (8.2%).[4] Italian companies also try to increase their profit margins by seeking out cheap production hubs – not only abroad, but also within Italy itself. In Tuscany, specifically in the Prato District, a cluster of low-cost manufacturing facilities has been established. Most of the workers there are Asian immigrants, who have to work in poor conditions, with low wages, little protection against unwarranted dismissal, and no job security. It is not just these particular workers who are enduring the negative consequences of the growth of this cheap industry: the result is that wages and prices are undercut and, thereby, constantly being reduced throughout the entire industry.[5]

From Brazilian cows to Italian shoes

A leather shoe 'made in Italy' often starts its journey in Brazil, South America's giant, which is one of the world's top producers of raw leather from cowhides – second only to the USA. As such, it is one of the Italian shoe industry's most important suppliers. Raw leather is a waste product from the resource-intensive meat industry. One of the largest multinational leather companies is the Brazilian corporation JBS S.A. (José Batista Sobrinho Sociedade Anónima), which is also one of the world's largest meat producers. Every day the company slaughters 100,000 cows, 70,000 pigs and 25,000 sheep. The hides and skins are processed in 26 different tanneries – in Brazil, Argentina, China, Germany, Italy, Mexico, South Africa, Vietnam and Uruguay – to obtain the end product, leather.[6] The bulk of this goes on to China, Italy and the USA.[7]

Preparing leather for shoe production is a multi-step process. Turning a raw hide into leather means removing the animal's hair and flesh, then pickling it (acidifying the pelt in an alkaline solution), in preparation for tanning. A by-product of these processes is a large amount of very toxic waste water and materials that are harmful to the environment and, critically, for the (tannery) workers handling them. In terms of the leather processed in the EU, this stage of production generally takes place in Italy – the country's leather production accounts for 60% of the European total.[8] In the Santa Croce District (in Italy's Venetian region) alone, there are 240 tanneries, where a mainly immigrant work-force carries out the hard, physical labour in dire conditions. A study from the Italian Clean Clothes Campaign (CCC) showed that, between 2009 and 2013, a total of 720 tannery workplace accidents occurred. Generally, the workers are not employed permanently or on a long-term basis, but instead through agencies on short, fixed-term or 'four-hour contracts'. This makes it hard for them to claim their employee rights and obtain even a minimum level of social security entitlements.[9]

The chemicals used in the tanning industry are particularly dangerous. Up until the beginning of the 20th century, it was common practice to use vegetable-based tannins, but that method was a lengthy one, which took a number of months. Nowadays, around 80% of leather is tanned using chemicals, which speeds up the process immensely.[10] The chemical most frequently utilised is chromium III salts, which completes the tanning process in less than a day. However, using chromium III can lead to the formation of unwanted chromium VI compounds – a substance that is absorbed through the skin, is allergenic and carcinogenic. The tannery workers are often unaware that they are being exposed to such a health risk, as are the people who wear the end products.

Chromium-tanned leather goes through a number of subsequent processes, including neutralisation, retanning, dyeing, fat liquoring and finishing. These production stages also involve the use of many different hazardous chemicals and salts. Muscular diseases, cancers, obstructive respiratory disorders and skin diseases top the list of tannery workers' most common health complaints.

To curb these negative effects, the EU introduced a new regulation on 1st May 2015, limiting the concentration of chromium VI allowed in leather articles sold in the EU to a maximum of 3 mg/kg.[11] It remains to be seen whether this law will in fact bring about sweeping changes and actually result in positive changes for tannery workers in terms of health and safety standards.

Costly stages of the production process are also often outsourced to Eastern European countries. According to the Albanian Office for National Statistics, over 80% of shoe and clothing exports manufactured in Albania are sent to Italy.[12] Production businesses in EU countries such as Romania, or non-EU countries such as Bosnia and Herzegovina, also act as suppliers for Italian companies. 'Outward processing' is the term used for this trade system, where precut pattern pieces for clothing or shoes are transported to another country, where they are sewn together and re-imported back. Since the collapse of the Soviet Union in 1991, the role of the garment and shoe industry in post-socialist Europe has been more or less limited to providing cheap, small-scale sewing facilities. These countries were de-industrialised and are now reliant on orders from West European purchasers, with a lack of any more extensive type of value creation there. The outward processing system is a dead-end street for the national economies, because a factory that relies solely on orders from abroad is completely dependent on buyers' deciding to use their services.[13]

Shoes – far from a disposable product

Shoes travel with us wherever we go and protect us from harm, from heat or cold. But shoes – just like clothes – are no longer merely about functionality; they have become sought after, and therefore lucrative, fashion items. To attract customers and increase their urge to consume, large corporations like H&M or Inditex (Zara and others) have chosen the well-engineered business model that is 'fast fashion': with an ever-changing product range, no fashion trend is missed. Designer pieces, presented on Fashion Week's runways, are copied and available in stores within a few weeks at a fraction of the price. This strategy is, among other things, boasted by celebrity endorsement deals and collaborations. Both H&M and Inditex produce shoes as well as clothes, and fast fashion – the quick, cheap and transient consumption of garments – is also well-established in the shoe sector.

The amount of shoes produced worldwide increased by almost 16% within the four-year period, 2011-2015.[14] The USA and Europe buy more shoes than any other regions and, in 2014, a total of 23.5 billion euros were spent on shoes in the EU.[15] Companies and shareholders profit from this growth, but the people who actually make our shoes are left wanting: they earn next to none of the brands' proceeds from sales. If a pair of shoes costs 120 € in a shop, for instance, factory workers see approximately 2.50 € of that.[16] Tannery workers are in a similar situation.

Making a living from new shoes is often a struggle

The stories of Mira, Sanja and Ilena[17] demonstrate that working conditions are intolerable in Eastern Europe, as well as in Asia. The three women described their average working day producing shoes for Western brands during research interviews carried out by the CCC in late 2015. What is particularly alarming is the extremely low wages they receive and the resulting problems associated with living in poverty.

Mira, Albania
"Working with a bit of dignity" – is all that Mira wishes for. She works in a shoe factory, six days a week, eight hours a day – sometimes more. After her hour-long journey to work on foot, she spends most of her time in front of a machine. Mira earns less than the legal minimum wage, around 20,000 lek (145 €) per month. She says that she has to feed her family of four with this amount, even though her earnings do not even cover her own needs. Because of this, she is getting deeper and deeper into debt. To make matters worse, her boss swears at the workers, pressurises them and shows them no respect.

Sanja, Macedonia
Sanja works for a factory that produces shoes for various companies, including well-known brands in Germany and Switzerland. In the high season, she works from 5am to 5pm, often even on national holidays. She earns between 12,000 (195 €) and 14,000 (227 €) denar per month. She says that she would actually need five times this much to be able to support her family. She has sometimes had her wages docked, without any explanation. The factory work tires her out too much for her to take on a second job. Because she has been working in the shoe factory for many years, being exposed to all the chemicals, glues and pastes there, she now suffers from allergies and respiratory problems.

Ilena, Romania
Ilena has worked for German and Austrian shoe brands in a Romanian shoe factory for 12 years. Her husband

China is by far the largest producer of shoes in the world. Seamstresses in a shoe factory in Hefei in the province of Anhui.

also works in a shoe factory. Both of them earn the monthly minimum wage (ca. 156 € net each). Their rent costs just under 89 € a month and they have to pay a further 81 € for electricity. "We try to live as simply and cheaply as possible. We can only afford the cheapest products," she explains. In order to be able to feed her family, she has a small vegetable garden and a few animals. Without this subsistence farming, they would not get by. Ilena dreams that one day she might be able to take take her children, aged 8 and 14, on holiday.

Shoes are valuable commodities: it is estimated that 25,000 litres of water and 50 m² of land are required to produce one pair of leather boots.[18] It follows then, that rapid production cycles and over-consumption have grave environmental impacts. Furthermore, excessive global production is exacerbated by low prices, which mean lower profit margins per product. Therefore, export-oriented countries try to offset this lower profit margin by higher volumes of production. In order to keep up with this development of the market, 'investor-friendly' laws are passed and minimum wages are kept low, with a great deal of overtime being worked as a matter of course in the industry.

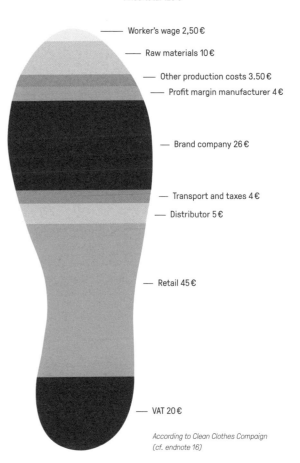

Price total 120 €

Worker's wage 2,50 €

Raw materials 10 €

Other production costs 3.50 €

Profit margin manufacturer 4 €

Brand company 26 €

Transport and taxes 4 €

Distributor 5 €

Retail 45 €

VAT 20 €

According to Clean Clothes Compaign (cf. endnote 16)

Salaries far below the living wage level are a problem in all manufacturing countries, including at factories based in Europe and, even, within the EU. The adverse health effects and potentially fatal consequences of a tannery environment are a grave cause for concern, as is the impact of chemicals, glues and pastes used in shoe factories. The current situation in the shoe industry means that labour and human rights abuses, serious health risks and environmental damage are the order of the day.

The **Clean Clothes Campaign** (CCC) is a global network committed to improving working conditions in the textile, garment and shoe industries. The network is made up of around 250 non-governmental organisations (NGOs) and trade unions worldwide, and has representatives in 17 European countries. In Switzerland, the work is coordinated by the **Berne Declaration** (BD) – a not-for-profit, independent organisation with around 25,000 members. For more than 40 years, the swiss NGO Berne Declaration has been campaigning for fairer partnerships between Switzerland and countries which are negatively impacted by globalisation.

Together with partners from the Clean Clothes Campaign, BD has launched a campaign to improve working conditions in the shoe industry. Their main demands are:

- a living wage for workers in the leather and shoe industry
- use of a tanning process that is safe for people and the planet
- sufficient health and safety protection for both tannery and factory workers
- more transparency about shoe production and working conditions in their supply chain, so that consumers can make more informed buying decisions.

Shopping for shoes more responsibly: what can I do?

Become a conscious consumer:
- Buy less: only buy shoes that you really need.
- Buy smart: only buy shoes that you can wear with the majority of your clothes.
- Buy shoes that, if needed, would be easy to repair.
- Gather more information before you go shopping, research companies that are making progress in all things 'fair'.

- If you are buying leather shoes, check whether the leather was tanned with a process that is environmentally and people friendly.
- Consider buying vegan shoes.
- Look out for shoes at jumble sales and in second-hand shops.
- Borrow shoes for special occasions that you are only going to wear once, from friends or rental services.
- Look after your shoes well, so that they last a long time.

Get involved and get active!

Ask favourite brands questions such as:
- Where is their leather sourced from? Call for supply chain transparency.
- What tanning process was used? Call for alternatives to chromium-tanned leather.
- How much do the workers in the tanneries, factories and retail shops earn? Call for a living wage for everyone employed in the supply chain.

Share your knowledge:
- Talk to your friends and colleagues about leather and shoes and tell them what you know about shoe manufacture. The more consumers there are calling for transparency, alternatives to chromium tanning and the provision of living wages for workers in the leather and shoe industry, the more things will start to change in the sector.

Join in the campaign:
- Get involved with CCC campaigns and/or take part in protest action (www.evb.ch; www.cleanclothes.ch).
- Find a related local BD activist group in your town or area.
- Organise a swap-shop for clothes and shoes and show others that there is another way to obtain these items.

1   World Footwear 2015.

2   World Footwear 2015

3   World Footwear 2015.

4   CBI Market Intelligence, Ministry of
    Foreign Affairs: 10.

5   Berne Declaration.

6   Corradini et al. 2015a: 3f.

7   Corradini et al. 2015b: 5.

8   Clean Clothes Campaign 2015.

9   Corradini et al. 2015a: 21, 26ff.

10 Corradini et al. 2015b: 14.

11 EUR-Lex.

12 INSTAT.

13 Luginbühl und Musiolek 2014: 19f.

14 2011: 21 billion pairs of shoes; 2015:
    24.3 billion pairs of shoes (World
    Footwear 2011; 2015).

15 CBI Market Intelligence, Ministry of
    Foreign Affairs 2015: 12.

16 The figures are based on a updated
    version of the CCC's calculation
    of value capture in the supply chain
    of the retail price of a running
    shoe. This was based on case study
    examples and other crucial factors,
    such as the part that brokers play and
    the rising cost of production over
    the last few years, which were not in-
    cluded in the original CCC calcula-
    tion. The updated calculation was
    done as part of a Masters thesis
    at Hohenheim University (Faculty of
    Economics and Social Sciences).
    The case study examples were based
    on interviews with experts, car-
    ried out as research for the Masters
    thesis. Hohenheim University, 2013:
    Analysis of value capture in the
    global value chain using the example
    of sports goods/the sports industry.

17 To protect the workers, we have
    changed their names.

18 Burley 2015: 11–14.

Trading in second-hand clothes is a
global multi-million business.

Tabea Grob

From the wardrobe to the charity bag: old clothes as global merchandise

In Switzerland, a large proportion of discarded textiles ends up in charity collection bags and containers. Collection enterprises make sure that the old clothes and shoes get a second life – either as second-hand products or as recyclable raw material. The trade in textiles is a lucrative global business.

A Texaid sorting warehouse in
Switzerland. The company generated
around 6 million euros in 2014.

In order to provide space for new clothes in our wardrobes, a large amount of our clothes and shoes end up in charity collections. The Swiss are diligent clothes donators: according to the Federal Office for Environment, they collect around six kilograms of textiles per head every year. This adds up to an annual amount of approximately 50,000 tonnes.[1] From the ecological viewpoint, it absolutely makes sense not to throw old clothes away as household waste, but to hand them over for appropriate disposal

Collecting companies such as Texaid make an effort to clearly explain where people's donated clothes will be sent to, as seen on their collection containers.

or reuse in collection bags and containers. However, most donors are probably unclear about what exactly happens to their garments. The idea that old clothes will be given free to people in need comes from a time when charitable aid organisations still collected old clothes independently and delivered them directly to the needy. Although most collection enterprises inform people about the commercial aspect of their collections, and their relationship to charitable organisations, this idea is still widespread. As a matter of fact, however, people in Europe today donate so many clothes that charities could not possibly manage to collect, sort and transport it all.[2] Therefore, they are supported by commercial enterprises, which collect and sell the old clothes for them. Part of the profit they make is given back to the charitable organisations.

Today's second-hand collectors are mostly private businesses which can make good profits out of the old clothes. As well as Tell-Tex and I:Collect AG (I:CO), which are both part of the world-leading SOEX GROUP, Texaid is one of the key players in the trade of used Swiss garments. Texaid states that they have 70 percent of the market share.[3] Although Texaid is a commercial enterprise, six charitable organisations own half its shares: the Swiss Red Cross (SRK), the Winterhilfe, Caritas

Switzerland, Kolping Switzerland, Solidar Suisse, and the Swiss protestant church charity HEKS. In fact, these charities founded Texaid in 1978, since when it has collected, sorted and recycled used textiles and shoes for them. In 2014, Texaid earned about 6.5 million Swiss francs (5.9 million euros) for the charities, which represents approximately 80 percent of its profits.[4] Tell-Tex works with partners Swiss Berghilfe, the Pestalozzi Child-

ren's Foundation and the Swiss Union of the Paralysed,[5] which received a share of about 3.4 million Swiss francs (3.1 million euros) in 2014 from Tell-Tex's sales.[6]

Profitably disposing of goods

In Switzerland, a permit is required for textile collection, and the municipalities and cantons can decide who they allow to put containers in their area, so Texaid and Tell-Tex are in competition with each other to obtain these licences. Although they both also run street collections using donation bags, this only accounts for a small portion of all the donated clothes gathered. In 2014, Tell-Tex only gained about 10 percent of all their clothes through these street collections, with most of it coming from static containers.[7]

Texaid receives between 60 and 70 centimes (54 to 63 euro cents) to several Swiss francs per kilogram of sorted clothes, depending on their quality.[8] This makes the second-hand clothes venture worthwhile. It is a business that is likely to grow in the future, as people throw away more and more of their clothes and shoes. Thieves have also become aware of the value of old clothes, often taking high-quality garments from containers,

T-shirt, household textile or tropical? 50,000 tonnes of old clothes are collected in Switzerland every year.

stealing collection bags or distributing fake charity collection bags. Up to 1,000 tonnes of textiles are stolen every year, corresponding to a lost revenue of one million Swiss francs (904,000 euros).[9]

Transnational sorting

The reutilisation of old clothes and shoes is an international process, just like their manufacture. For financial reasons, most second-hand clothes are not sorted out in their country of origin, but sent abroad for this stage. Texaid and its German subsidiary, the Texaid Collection GmbH, collect a total of about 75,000 tonnes of used clothes per year, half of which is collected in Switzerland. Some of this is sorted in Apolda, Germany, and Schattdorf, Switzerland, where the enterprise has its head office. The rest is processed in sorting warehouses abroad: every year more than 6,000 tonnes in Bulgaria, 4,000 tonnes in Hungary, and over 9,000 tonnes in Tangier, Morocco. This location in the European-Moroccan free trade zone gives some important advantages to the businesses, which benefit from tax relief, cheaper workforces and closer geographical proximity to the African sales market.

A business model with an ecological contradiction

Nowadays, second-hand clothes can also be deposited into containers in some new clothing shops, an initiative begun by I:Collect AG. To encourage customers to donate more of their old clothes to I:CO's containers, fashion shops provide a voucher which can be exchanged for new clothes in-store, when a shopper donates an item, regardless of its brand, quality or condition. For example, if a shopper donates an old pair of pyjamas at the Italian lingerie store Intimissimi, they will receive a voucher for three Swiss francs (2.71 euros), which can be redeemed against a purchase of 15 Swiss francs (13.56 euros) or more. As well as Intimissimi, other major fashion chains like H&M, C&A, Mammut, Puma, Vögele Shoes, Levi's and Transa, are also I:CO's partners in this venture.[10]

Donating to charities is part of I:CO's philosophy, as it is for most second-hand collectors. For every kilogram of clothes that I:CO collects, it gives 0.02 euros to the fundraiser Charity Star, which was set up on the Internet by I:CO.[11] Charity Star asks users to vote for various charitable projects on its homepage. If I:CO donates 1,000 euros – which is equivalent to 50 tonnes of clothes being collected in their containers – the project with the most votes is given that amount. Unfortunately, I:CO does not state how long it takes to reach this amount.

Although the fashion stores are ostensibly demonstrating their environmental consciousness by participating in I:CO's clothes collections, they are simultaneously encouraging further excessive consumption by giving out a voucher that should trigger an incentive to buy. I:CO advertises its take-back system by stating that it will reduce the amount of textiles thrown away as rubbish by recycling, however, it contradicts its own claim of sustainability through the inducement to buy more replacement pieces. I:CO points out how big the volume of water consumption and CO_2 emission for the production of a T-shirt is, asserting that these resources can be spared by recycling.[12] At the same time, however, the discount vouchers serve to boost the revenue of the shops involved. In this way, the old textiles remain in the consumer cycle through recycling, but the earth's limited raw materials are exploited further by the voucher system which increases consumerism.

Second-hand boutique or shredder?

The sorting process is essential for the collection businesses, because correctly classifying the textiles can maximise their profit. Texaid and Tell-Tex stress that 65 percent of their items find new owners as second-hand clothes, although only an average of 45 to 50 percent are resold as garments.[13] Unsellable old clothes are processed further, either into cleaning rags or by being recycled into fibres. Buttons and other metal applications are removed, then the clothes are chopped up and divided into fibres with a shredder.[14] This raw material can than be processed into, for example, insulation material for the automobile industry.

Used shoes are also sorted out, according to whether they are still wearable or not. If not, they end up in the waste incineration plant. It is not yet possible to recycle shoes, because materials like leather, rubber or plastics are often stuck together and impossible to seperate from each other. This is an issue that the SOEX GROUP would like to change with their first shoe-recycling machine, which should begin running at the end of 2016.[15] The materials acquired by this could be reused as recycling material for doormats, belts or rubber soles for new shoes.[16]

Textiles, which are considered valuable, are first divided in the sorting plant into rough categories and then into increasingly more specific groupings, until they are eventually classified by up to 200 categories. These include, for example, 'swimming clothes', 'baby clothes', 'socks' or 'tropical'. 'Tropical' is one of Texaid's categories, which describes light clothing with slight defects which are destined primarily for outlets in Africa.[17] The final fine-screening of the textiles is complicated and elaborate, because their cataloguing criteria includes a combination of different factors: the quality and condition of the clothes and their materials play a role, as does the style of fashion, their brand and fit with country-specific buying preferences. This clothes classification is carried out by workers who are each assigned to single steps in the sorting process. Within seconds, they must decide which category a garment on the conveyor belt belongs to. Therefore, their visual perception is very important, as well as their tactile sensory perception, because the clothes' material is a crucial element of their categorisation.

The best-quality items are called cream, in the jargon of used clothes traders.[18] Such branded products in good condition can be resold profitably in Switzerland itself. For example, Texaid offers high-quality used clothes

A second-hand boutique of Caritas in Zurich: The best quality can be resold in its country of origin – the worst goes to Africa.

for sale under the name 'shoshop', through the platform ricardo.ch. There, for example, a Hugo Boss blazer is on sale for 99 Swiss francs (89.50 euros).[19] While the condition of this article is described as 'used', no information can be found on ricardo.ch to explain that it is reselling textiles from collection containers or that Texaid is behind the enterprise.

According to FairWertung e.V., the German trade association for charitable clothes collectors, the cream only represents about 12 percent of the clothes collected in Germany,[20] but it accounts for most of their income. Slightly lower-quality items are sold by the Swiss exporters to Eastern Europe, and the worst garments are exported to African countries, where the lowest prices are paid.

Interview with Martin Böschen, CEO of Texaid

Tabea Grob: *Why aren't old clothes given for free to people in need?*
Martin Böschen: Texaid collects more than 140 million garments every year. These clothes must be sorted and classified, which costs money. If old clothes were handed over free of charge to people in need, these costs would not be covered. Only roughly 20 percent of the collected old clothes make more money from sales than the costs of collecting and sorting. The sales of this so-called cream must cover the costs of further processing the remaining 80 percent.

How much can 1 kilogram of old clothes be sold for?
1 kilogram of clothes corresponds to about three and a half to four garments, and can be sold to middlemen for between 60 centimes and several Swiss francs. The price depends on the quality of the clothes. Old clothes of the highest quality can be sold for five and a half to six and a half Swiss francs a kilo, this results in roughly 2 Swiss francs per garment. But it is not just the quality which is crucial. Men's clothes are, in general, more expensive because they only represent about 20 percent of the clothes collected. Women seem to change their clothes more often and are more likely to give them away to clothes collections. Therefore, Texaid has a surplus of ladies' wear.

Does Texaid resell the old clothes directly to the end consumer?
Texaid sells the old textiles from the sorting plant directly to importers from different countries. We have

no single main buyer or a particular country to which many old textiles are imported. Thereby the risk of losing a customer can be decreased.

The recycling of used shoes is not yet possible at the moment. Do many shoes therefore end up in the rubbish?
Not necessarily. Unlike clothes, we can still resell shoes if they only have small, easily repairable damage like, for example, a loose sole. Shoe manufacture is costlier than clothes and, therefore, it is worth doing this repair work.

Is there real competition for the old clothes in African countries?
At the beginning of the 2000s, cheap new products imported from Asia provided competition to the old clothes at the African markets. Nevertheless, due to the better quality, many traders turned back to West European old clothes after two or three years. Moreover, these clothes create work for many people, for instance by adapting them or distributing them. Such possibilities do not arise with the imported products from Asia.

By the tonne: a global trade in old clothes

After being sorted out, the clothes are pressed into 50-kilogram bales and wrapped up in waterproof plastic.[21] They are then transported inside containers on cargo ships, to the target countries all over the world. According to the Trans-Americas Trading Company,[22] a standard large container called a '40' High-Cube' container (2.4 metres wide, 2.6 metres high and 12.2 metres long), can carry 450 bales of clothes.

According to UN Comtrade Database data, the USA exports more second-hand textiles than any other country, sending over 773,000 tonnes all over the world in 2014.[23] Europe's used clothes exports are often handled via places with harbour access and colonial-historical relations to the recipient countries.[24] An example is the Netherlands, which was the sixth largest exporter in the world, according to the UN Comtrade's 2014 statistics. In fact, not all of the old clothes that are shipped via Dutch harbours come from the Netherlands, many are from neighbouring areas. The following UN Comtrade statistics do not distinguish which garments are shipped from their donor country from those which are only in transit through the exporting country. Therefore, the numbers must be reviewed with caution, but they

The clothes are packed
into plastic bales and shipped
to their destinations.

nevertheless give an approximate picture of the global used clothes trade.

In 2014, more than 4 million tonnes of old clothes were exported worldwide.[25] The six most important exporters, according to the UN Comtrade statistics, exported about 55 percent of the total volume. However, their overall share has decreased over recent years, since more and more countries have started trading global second-hand clothes, particularly some Asian countries, which are relatively new and successful exporters.

Switzerland exported roughly 60,000 tonnes in 2014, so is ranked 16th in used clothes trade worldwide. The Federal Office for Environment estimates that each

Swiss citizen donates approximately 6 kilograms of old clothes per year, while the UN Comtrade figure puts it even higher, at 7 kilograms. Either way, the amount of clothes donated is unexpectedly high, considering the size of Switzerland's population. The reasons for this might be, on the one hand, the wealthy Swiss populace's propensity to consume or, on the other hand, their high levels of environmental consciousness and recycling diligence.

Are there alternatives to the commercial trade of old clothes?

The sale of old clothes ensures that still wearable clothes are not pointlessly thrown away as rubbish, but continue to be used. The trade generates jobs, earns profits, and shares some of these with charitable organisations. But not all collection enterprises provide transparent information about the structure of their business. If consumers and donors are not enlightened about the further use of their garments, the false belief that their old clothes will be given free to needy people will remain, to the benefit of the commercial businesses. Some unscrupulous organisations even exploit

Source:
UN Comtrade Database

EXPORTING COUNTRY		EXPORT OF SECOND-HAND TEXTILES IN TONNES
1.	USA	773 817
2.	Germany	494 773
3.	Great Britain	351 788
4.	Republic of Korea	307 798
5.	Japan	239 914
6.	Netherlands	158 405
16.	Switzerland	60 000

people's charitable motives to achieve profits for themselves, without any approval from, or relation to, charities.

This uncertainty about their activities is not new for collection enterprises. The German Red Cross is keen to provide better clarification and, in a 2012 transparency initiative, it added stickers to all its old clothes collection containers which provided information about how the donated clothes would be used, explaining that most of it would be resold.[26] This gives donors the responsibility of deciding whether they consider this approach to be reasonable or not. The German umbrella organisation FairWertung e.V. is also advocating an increased transparency of process, and its members adhere to certain standards which inform donors about how their old clothes will be used and resold.[27] However, the main German clothes collectors, such as SOEX GROUP or HUMANA, do not belong to this umbrella organisation.

Anyone wishing to hand over their used, but still intact, clothes as a genuine donation to people in need, should turn to clothing shops. The charitable organisation Caritas Switzerland – a partner of Texaid – provides an alternative to the commercial used clothes trade. Textiles in good condition that are given directly to this charity end up in the clothes store in Waldibrücke near Lucerne, where people in need, like asylum seekers or refugees, can profit from their low prices.[28] The charitable organisation Schweizer Berghilfe, a partner of Tell-Tex, collects explicitly for people in need too. Tell-Tex's package service delivers garments in good condition free of charge to people living in the Swiss mountains.[29]

1 BAFU 2015.

2 Wagener-Böck 2015: 205.

3 Texaid 2015.

4 Ibid.

5 Tell-Tex 2015.

6 Ibid.

7 Ibid.

8 Interview with Martin Böschen, CEO of Texaid, on 9 February 2016.

9 Schoop 2014.

10 I:CO.

11 Ibid.

12 Ibid.

13 Texaid and Tell-Tex.

14 DocumentaryTuber.

15 Wahnbaeck 2015.

16 Ibid.

17 Yafasia.

18 FairWertung.

19 ricardo.ch 2015.

20 FairWertung.

21 Hansen 2000: 110.

22 Trans-Americas Trading Company.

23 UN Comtrade Database.

24 Hansen 2000: 112.

25 UN Comtrade Database.

26 Deutsches Rotes Kreuz.

27 FairWertung.

28 Caritas Schweiz.

29 Tell-Tex.

After years in the shoe business, Chedo managed to build a room for his family in 2015. They still do not have electricity or running water.

Alexis Malefakis

Making a living from old shoes

Most of the shoe vendors have not been able to realise their dream of making a better life in the city. After many years in the business, the constant fear of being unable to provide for their families remains. Trading in old shoes is not a promising future prospect for them.

Whether considering a special offer at a discount store or purchasing a superior quality brand-name shoe, as conscious consumers today we know that we are often only able to enjoy our wealth and affluence at the expense of other people's opportunities in life. Granted, through the worldwide system of shoe production, people can gain employment and, thus, an opportunity to earn an income in tanning in Brazil or Bangladesh and sewing in Vietnam or Bulgaria. But they are forced to work and live in circumstances that none of their product's consumers would like to endure. Workers' rights, as they apply in countries like Switzerland or Germany, can easily be circumvented by outsourcing certain processes to low-wage countries, in order to minimise production costs. Many of the people manufacturing a company's products, however, benefit least from the bigger profit margins attained in this way.

The clothes and shoes that Westerners discard and donate to charity when they are still wearable provide the basis of transactions for an entire economic sector which employs thousands of people and delivers merchandise to several million second-hand traders in Africa and other world regions. But trading in old clothes and shoes offers only precarious economic prospects for the people at the lower end of the global chain, such as the shoe vendors in the streets of Dar es Salaam. Their impressive enthusiasm for their work cannot hide the fact that they live and work with the constant fear of being arrested by the police, jailed and even beaten up – or of simply being unable to sell enough to provide for their families. Moving on from street vending was a dream they all shared and often expressed towards me.

There were plenty of alternative ideas at the *kijiweni*. All of them considered that trade would be the most profitable option. As they told me, they already considered themselves to be experts in that field – but they dreamed of opening a shop rather than doing petty business as mobile vendors. They wanted to own a substantial stock of merchandise instead of just carrying four or five pairs of shoes in their hands. Above all, they dreamed about selling bigger quantities of goods and, thus, making larger profits than the two or three euros they made each day by selling shoes. More capital, a fixed address for their premises, higher sales and profits would give them a degree of socioeconomic security that would allow them and their families to live a life of modest prosperity.

What does 'modest prosperity' mean for them? The shoe vendors explained to me in interviews that

if, by some stroke of luck, they got hold of a larger sum of money, such as 500 or even 1,000 euros, they would try to build their own house, even if it consisted of just one room for the whole family. Having a place of their own would free them from the periodic problem of needing to pay six months' or an entire year's rent in advance, as is usual in Dar es Salaam. The 80 to 160 euros that this requires poses a serious problem to each of them, given the small daily profits they make. Or they would be able to pay secondary school fees for one of their children, including payments for school books, school uniforms, examination fees and lunches, instead of declaring that their education was over after seven years of primary school, because they cannot afford the 10 or 15 euros that a secondary school would cost every term.[1] Modest prosperity would also mean freedom from the fear that a family member might die of a disease that could be cured by medicine costing as little as 10 or 20 euros. Such basic life aspirations were the reason why the young men had left their homes in the first place and come to the city as economic 'refugees', settling in an initially unknown environment to seek a life of dignity and self-esteem.

However, most of the shoe vendors have not yet realised their dream of a better life in the city. Instead, they often expressed frustration at feeling stuck in a kind of gridlock situation, treading water without ever reaching anywhere. *'Maji yanafuata mkondo'*, the water follows the riverbed, they said, when we talked about their own and their children's future. They had come from poor backgrounds and their children were growing up equally poor. They had hardly enjoyed any education and their children will remain as uneducated as them.

Despite the many shiny skyscrapers in the city centre and the increasing number of expensive cars cruising through the streets, the country's economic development appears to simply bypass people like the shoe vendors. There is a small elite who profit from Tanzania's wealth in natural resources, but most of the population hardly gain any benefits from its reputed economic growth.

In stark contrast, business opportunities in second-hand shoes are declining in Dar es Salaam. It is becoming ever more difficult to find suitable shoes for sale at Karume Market, since more inferior quality merchandise is being imported from Asia which is difficult to sell in the streets. In addition, the city's population's constant growth is leading to increasing numbers of young men trying to earn their livelihood in the streets. Simultaneously, due to the city's construction boom, suitable vending areas are being replaced by high-rise buildings and shopping malls which are guarded by private security guards instructed to defend the premises against 'loitering' street vendors.

Making a living from selling old shoes is possible – but it leads to a life of poverty which lacks any kind of security or future prospects. As Christa Luginbühl has shown, it is equally difficult for people to make a living by producing new shoes. Global production, consumption and trade in clothes and shoes thus connects people who live on different continents and in vastly differing conditions. In that sense, globalisation really is bringing us closer to one another, but our relations are marked by a significant differential in power and prosperity. The over-consumption of a few is facilitated by the efforts of many others who work in conditions that would be intolerable to the products' consumers. Cheap production of our consumer goods is coterminous with poverty-level wages and lack of personal security for workers and their families. So, if each donation of used clothes is followed by a new purchase of throwaway fashion or even branded goods, we have little reason to feel good about our generosity.

For many people in Tanzania and other countries, discarded clothes and shoes from the West are both a boon and a bane. Brand new consumer items such as a new pair of Levi's jeans or Adidas trainers are completely unaffordable for most. Because of their subsistence or, sometimes, almost non-existent incomes, many people in Dar es Salaam are keen to buy second-hand clothes and shoes from Asia, the USA and Europe. The people who trade in used goods – be they market traders, shop owners or street vendors – rely on imported *mitumba* as the basis of their business. At the same time, however, the saturation of the Tanzanian market with foreign second-hand goods means that local producers cannot compete with these cheap imports. This has already had a disastrous impact on the country's textile industries, and it would be extremely challenging to establish new industries in such circumstances. The major beneficiaries of this business model are not the street vendors who earn the oft-cited 'dollar a day' by reselling our discarded clothes and shoes. Instead of finding steady jobs in a sustainable industry, they are entirely dependent on the consumer waste of the rich world. Making a living from old shoes therefore means relying on the drip-feed from a global junk-economy, which exemplifies a creeping structural violence that we European consumers are only just beginning to understand.

---

1   At the time of the research, in 2011 to 2013, public secondary schools charged fees, and this was only stopped in February 2016. The numbers of new students have risen abruptly, which shows that many parents had previously wanted to send their children to school but not been able to afford to. At the same time, the high numbers of new students poses substantial new challenges to many chronically-underfunded schools (Lobulu 2016).

Authors

Mareile Flitsch is a social anthropologist and sinologist with a research focus on the anthropology of technology, culinary anthropology, popular architecture, practical knowledge and skilled practice and the anthropology of China. Since 2008, she has been professor for social anthropology at the ISEK (Institut für Sozialanthropologie und Empirische Kulturwissenschaft, Institute for Social Anthropology and Empirical Cultural Studies) and the director of the Ethnographic Museum at the University of Zurich.

Alexis Malefakis is a social anthropologist with a research focus on urban anthropology, economic anthropology, praxeology and material culture, and a regional focus on sub-Saharan Africa. He gained his doctoral degree from the University of Constance with a dissertation on street vendors in Dar es Salaam, Tanzania. Since 2014, he has been the curator of the African collections at the Ethnographic Museum at the University of Zurich.

Christa Luginbühl has worked for the NGO Berne Declaration (BD) since 2008 and is responsible for coordinating the Clean Clothes Campaign (CCC) in Switzerland. Her work focuses on corporate responsibility and the enforcement of workers' and human rights in global supply chains. She does research into the living conditions of factory workers in the clothes and shoe industry, organises campaigns and coordinates policies for the international CCC-network.

Tabea Grob is a social anthropology student at the University of Zurich. Her regional focus is on Central Asia and Africa. Her thematic focus is on questions of globalisation and north-south relations.

Bibliography

Appadurai, Arjun: *Modernity at Large. Cultural Dimensions of Globalization*, 3rd printing, (Public Worlds; vol. 1), Minneapolis 1997.

Archer, Margaret S.: Morphogenesis versus Structuration: on Combining Structure and Action, in: *The British Journal of Sociology*, vol. 33, no. 4, Oxford 1982, pp. 455–483.

Bernard, H. Russell: *Research Methods in Anthropology. Qualitative and Quantitative Approaches*, 5th ed., Lanham MD 2011.

Bloch, Maurice: Language, Anthropology and Cognitive Science, in: *Man*, n.s., vol. 26, no. 1–2, London 1991, pp. 183–198.

Bourdieu, Pierre: *Entwurf einer Theorie der Praxis auf der ethnologischen Grundlage der kabylischen Gesellschaft*, Frankfurt am Main 1976 [french 1972].

Bourdieu, Pierre: *Sozialer Sinn. Kritik der theoretischen Vernunft*, (Suhrkamp-Taschenbuch Wissenschaft; 1066), Frankfurt am Main 1987 [french 1980].

Bourdieu, Pierre: *Pascalian Meditations*, Cambridge 2000 [french 1997].

Brennan, James R. and Burton, Andrew: The Emerging Metropolis: a history of Dar es Salaam, circa 1862-2000, in: Brennan, James R., Burton, Andrew and Lawi, Yusuf (eds.): *Dar es Salaam. Histories from an emerging African metropolis*, Dar es Salaam 2007, pp. 13–75.

Brown, Alison, Lyons, Michal and Dankoco, Ibrahima: Street Traders and the Emerging Spaces for Urban Voice and Citizenship in African Cities, in: *Urban Studies*, vol. 47, no. 3, London 2010, pp. 666–683.

Burton, Andrew: *African Underclass. Urbanisation, Crime & Colonial Order in Dar es Salaam*, Oxford 2005.

Burton, Andrew: Raw Youth, School-Leavers and the Emergence of Structural Unemployment in Late-Colonial Urban Tanganyika, in: *The Journal of African History*, vol. 47, no. 3, Cambridge 2006, pp. 363–387.

Burton, Andrew: The Haven of Peace Purged: Tackling the Undesirable and Unproductive Poor in Dar es Salaam, ca. 1950s–1980s, in: *The International Journal of African Historical Studies*, vol. 40, no. 1, Boston 2007, pp. 119–151.

Costello, Matthew J.: Administration Triumphs over Politics: the Transformation of the Tanzanian State, in: *African Studies Review*, vol. 39, no. 1, Cambridge 1996, pp. 123–148.

Dewalt, Kathleen M. and Dewalt, Billie R.: *Participant Observation. A Guide for Fieldworkers*, 2nd ed., Lanham MD 2011.

Dougherty, Janet W. D. and Keller, Charles M.: Taskonomy: a practical approach to knowledge structures, in: *American Ethnologist*, vol. 9, no. 4, Arlington TX 1982, pp. 763–774.

Fabian, Johannes: *Time and the Other. How Anthropology Makes its Object*, New York 1983.

Flitsch, Mareile: *Des Menschen Fertigkeit. Ethnologische Perspektiven einer neuen Wertschät-*

zung praktischen Wissens = On Human Skill. Anthropological Perspectives on a New Appreciation of Practical Knowledge, Zurich 2014.

Frazer, Gareth: Used-Clothing Donations and Apparel Production in Africa, in: *The Economic Journal*, vol. 118, issue 532, Oxford 2008, pp. 1764–1784.

Giddens, Anthony: *Central Problems in Social Theory. Action, Structure and Contradiction in Social Analysis*, Berkeley CA 1979.

Giddens, Anthony: *Die Konstitution der Gesellschaft. Grundzüge einer Theorie der Strukturierung*, 3. Aufl., (Theorie und Gesellschaft; Bd. 1), Frankfurt am Main 1997 [engl. 1984].

Hansen, Karen Tranberg: *Salaula. The World of secondhand clothing and Zambia*, Chicago 2000.

Hart, Keith: Informal Income Opportunities and Urban Employment in Ghana, in: *The Journal of Modern African Studies*, vol. 11, no. 1, Cambridge 1973, pp. 61–89.

Hirschauer, Stefan: Puttings Things into Words. Ethnographic Description and the Silence of the Social, in: *Human Studies* vol. 29, no. 4, 2006, pp. 413–441.

Höft, Michael: Das Kilo für 1,20 Dollar. Das grosse Geschäft mit den Kleiderspenden aus Deutschland, in: *Die Zeit*, Nr. 45, 3. November 2011, pp. 1-2.

Hütz-Adams, Friedel: *Kleider machen Beute. Deutsche Altkleider vernichten afrikanische Arbeitsplätze*. Eine Studie, (Texte / Südwind, Institut für Ökonomie und Ökumene; 5), Siegburg 1995.

Iliffe, John: *A Modern History of Tanganyika*, (African Studies Series; 25), Cambridge 1979.

Ingold, Tim: *The Perception of the Environment. Essays on livelihood, dwelling and skill, reprint*, London 2007.

Ingold, Tim: *Being Alive. Essays on movement, knowledge and description*, London 2011.

International Labour Organization (ed.): *Measuring Informality. A statistical manual on the informal sector and informal employment*, Geneva 2013a.

International Labour Organization (ed.): *Women and Men in the Informal Economy: a Statistical Picture*, 2nd ed., Geneva 2013b.

Ivanov, Paola: Aneignung. Der museale Blick als Spiegel der europäischen Begegnung mit Afrika, in: Arndt, Susan (Hrsg.): *AfrikaBilder. Studien* pp. 351–371.

Keller, Charles M. and Keller, Janet Dixon: *Cognition and Tool Use. The Blacksmith at Work*, Cambridge 1996.

Leslie, John A. K.: *A Survey of Dar es Salaam*, London 1963.

Lugalla, Joe L. P.: Development, Change, and Poverty in the Informal Sector during the Era of Structural Adjustments in Tanzania, in: *Canadian Journal of African Studies = Revue Canadienne des Études Africaines*, vol. 31, no. 3, Abingdon 1997, pp. 424–451.

Luvanga, Nathanael E.: Towards the Development of Informal Sector Policy in Tanzania: Some Policy Issues, in: University of Dar es Salaam, Economic Research Bureau (ed.): *ERB Paper*, n.s., no. 95.1, Dar es Salaam 1996.

Lyons, Michal, Brown, Alison and Msoka, Colman: (Why) have pro-poor policies failed Africa's working poor? in: *Journal of International Development*, vol. 24, Chichester 2012, pp. 1008–1029.

Lyons, Michal and Msoka, Colman Titus: The World Bank and the Street: (How) Do "Doing Business" Reforms Affect Tanzania's Micro-traders? in: *Urban Studies*, vol. 47, no. 5, London 2010, pp. 1079–1097.

MacGaffey, Janet and Bazenguissa-Ganga, Rémy: *Congo – Paris. Transnational Traders on the Margins of the Law*, London 2000.

Malefakis, Alexis: Fremde Dinge: die Rezeption Afrikanischer Kunst als kulturelle Aneignung, in: *Münchner Beiträge zur Völkerkunde. Jahrbuch des Staatlichen Museums für Völkerkunde München*, Bd. 13, München 2009, pp. 93–116.

Malefakis, Alexis: Rewarding Frictions: Fieldwork and Street Vending in Dar es Salaam, in: *Zeitschrift für Ethnologie*, vol. 140, Berlin, pp. 177–189.

Marcus, George E.: Ethnography in/of the World System: the Emergence of Multi-Sited Ethnography, in: *Annual Review of Anthropology*, vol. 24, Palo Alto CA 1995, pp. 95–117.

Mbilinyi, Marjorie: "City" and "Countryside" in Colonial Tanganyika, in: *Economic and Political Weekly*, vol. 20, no. 43, Mumbai (Bombay) 1985, pp. WS88–WS96.

Msoka, Colman Titus: *Informal Markets and Urban Development: a Study of Street Vending in Dar es Salaam, Tanzania*, (Dissertation Abstracts International. Section A; vol. 66–10), Minnesota 2005, zugl. Diss. Univ. of Minnesota, 2005.

National Bureau of Statistics (Tanzania), Ministry of Labour, Youth Development and Sports (ed.): *Integrated Labour Force Survey 2000/2001*, Dar es Salaam 2002.

National Bureau of Statistics (Tanzania), Ministry of Finance and Office of Chief Government Statistician President's Office, Finance, Economy and Development Planning (eds.): *2012 Population and Housing Census. Population Distribution by Administrative Areas*, Dar es Salaam 2013.

Newell, Sasha: *The Modernity Bluff. Crime, Consumption, and Citizenship in Côte d'Ivoire*, Chicago 2012.

Rivoli, Pietra: *The Travels of a T-Shirt in the Global Economy. An Economist Examines the Markets, Power, and Politics of World Trade*, Hoboken NJ 2005.

Schoop, Florian: Die Altkleiderdiebe. Mit unseren alten Stoffen wird Profit gemacht – auch mit illegalen Mitteln, in: *Neue Zürcher Zeitung*, Nr. 34, 11.02.2014, pp. 12.

Simone, AbdouMaliq: *For the City yet to Come. Changing African Life in Four Cities*, Durham NC 2004.

Triche, Thelma: *A Case Study of Public-Private and Public-Public Partnerships in Water Supply and Sewerage Services in Dar es Salaam*, (Water Papers; no. 69032), Washington DC 2012.

United Nations Human Settlements Programme (ed.): *The State of African Cities 2014. Re-imagining Sustainable Urban Transitions*, (UN-Habitat series; 3), Nairobi 2014.

Wagener-Böck, Nadine: "Nachhaltiges" Weitertragen? Überlegungen zum humanitären Hilfsgut Altkleider zwischen Überfluss und Begrenzung, in: Tauschek, Markus und Grewe, Maria (Hrsg.): *Knappheit, Mangel, Überfluss. Kulturwissenschaftliche Positionen zum Umgang mit begrenzten Ressourcen*, Frankfurt am Main 2015, pp. 205–225.

Whorf, Benjamin Lee: *Sprache – Denken - Wirklichkeit. Beiträge zur Metalinguistik und Sprachphilosophie*, 99.–102. Tsd., (Rowohlts Enzyklopädie; 403), Reinbek bei Hamburg 1988 [engl. 1956].

Internet sources

BAFU (Bundesamt für Umwelt, Schweiz): *Kleider und Schuhe*, URL: http://www.bafu.admin.ch/abfall/01472/01860/index.html?lang=de [Date of access: 3.11.2015].

Berne Declaration (BD): *Made in Italy*, URL: https://www.evb.ch/themen-hintergruende/konsum/mode/existenzlohn/made-in-italy [Date of access: 4.2.2016].

Burley, Helen: *Mind your step. The land and water footprints of everyday products*, London 2015, URL:https://www.foe.co.uk/sites/default/files/downloads/mind-your-step-report-76803.pdf [Date of access: 4.2.2016].

Caritas Schweiz: *Kleider spenden*, URL: https://www.caritas.ch/de/aktiv-werden/kleider-spenden [Date of access: 10.11.2015].

CBI Market Intelligence, Ministry of Foreign Affairs: *CBI Trade Statistics: Footwear sector in Europe*, Den Haag 2015, URL: https://www.cbi.eu/sites/default/files/trade-statistics-europe-foot-wear-2015.pdf [Date of access: 4.2.2016].

Clean Clothes Campaign: *Wie kommt der Schuh unter den Christbaum?* Wien 2015, URL: http://cleanclothes.at/de/presse/wie-kommt-der-schuh-unter-den-christbaum [Date of access: 4.2.2016].

Corradini, Pierpaolo, Gallo, Stefano and Gesualdi, Francesco: *A Tough Story of Leather. A journey into the tanning industry via the Santa Croce District*, Vecchiano 2015a, URL: http://www.cleanclothes.at/media/common/uploads/download/bericht-a-tough-story-of-leather/FAIR%20-%20Change%20your%20shoes%20ENG.pdf [Date of access: 4.2.2016].

Corradini, Pierpaolo, Gallo, Stefano and Gesualdi, Francesco: *Did You Know there's a Cow in Your Shoe? The labor and the environment behind a pair of leather shoes*, Vecchiano 2015b, URL: https://www.global2000.at/sites/global/files/FAIR%20%20did%20you%20know%20theres%20a%20cow%20in%20your%20shoe.compressed.pdf [Date of access: 4.2.2016].

DocumentaryTuber: *[DOKU] Die AltKleider-Mafia – 2013*, Youtube.com 07.05.2013, URL: https://www.youtube.com/watch?v=ZXSubzw6tCo [Date of access: 3.11.2015].

Deutsches Rotes Kreuz: *Transparenz-Initiative Altkleider*, URL: http://www.drk.de/aktuelles/fokus-themen/kleidersammlung.html [Date of access: 4.12.2015].

EUR-Lex: *Commission Regulation (EU) No 301/2014 of 25 March 2014*, URL: http://eur-lex.europa.eu/legal-content/EN/TXT/?uri=CELEX%3A32014R0301 [Date of access: 4.2.2016].

FairWertung: *FairWertung bewusst handeln*, URL: http://www.fairwertung.de/index.html [Date of access: 4.12.2015].

I:Collect: *Charity Star*, URL: http://www.ico-spirit.com/de/charitystar [Date of access: 3.11.2015].

INSTAT (Instituti i Statistikave, Tiranë), URL: http://www.instat.gov.al/en/Home.aspx [Date of access: 4.2.2016].

Kinabo, Oliva D.: *The Textile Industry and the Mitumba Market in Tanzania. A Paper presented to the Tanzania-Network.de Conference on Textile Market and Textile Industry in Rural and Urban Areas in Tanzania on 23rd October 2004 in Potsdam-Germany*, Dar es Salaam 2004, URL: http://www.tanzaniagateway.org/docs/textile_industry_and_the_mitumba_market_in_tanzania.pdf [Date of access: 17.2.2016].

Lobulu, William: Tanzania: Snag in "Free Education" Could Have Been Avoided, in: *Arusha Times*, 6 February 2016, URL: http://allafrica.com/stories/201602082493.html [Date of access: 25.2.2016].

Luginbühl, Christa and Musiolek, Bettina: *Im Stichgelassen: die Armutslöhne der Arbeiterinnen in Kleiderfabriken in Osteuropa und der Türkei. Report 2014*, URL: https://www.evb.ch/fileadmin/files/documents/CCC/2014_D_CCC-Report-Stitched_Up.pdf [Date of access: 4.2.2016].

Ricardo.ch: *Suisse-deluxe*, URL: https://www.ricardo.ch/online-shop/suisse-deluxe/?SortingType=2&SellerNickName=suisse-deluxe&PriceMax=110&PriceMin=80 [Date of access: 20.1.2016].

Sturgis, Sam: The Bright Future of Dar es Salaam, an Unlikely African Megacity, in: *Citylab*, 25 February 2015, URL: http://www.citylab.com/design/2015/02/the-bright-future-of-dar-es-salaam-an-unlikely-african-megacity/385801 [Date of access: 20.11.2015].

Tell-Tex: *Kleidersammlung Schweiz*, URL: http://tell-tex.ch [Date of access: 3.11.2015].

Texaid: *Gebrauchte Textilien – Rohstoffe für Neues*, URL: http://www.texaid.ch/de [Date of access: 3.11.2015].

Trans-Americas Trading Company: *Purchasing, processing, recycling and sales of post-consumer textiles/secondhand clothing*, URL: http://www.tranclo.com [Date of access: 7.12.2015].

UN Comtrade Database: URL: http://comtrade.un.org/data [Date of access: 22.2.2016].

Wahnbaeck, Carolin: Schuh-Recycling: Alte Treter auf neuen Pfaden, in: *Spiegel Online*, 26.07.2015,

URL: http://www.spiegel.de/wirtschaft/
unternehmen/schuh-recycling-soex-versucht-
schuhe-wiederzuverwerten-a-1043163.html
[Date of access: 22.11.2015].

World Footwear: *World Footwear Yearbook 2011*, URL:
http://www.worldfootwear.com/store.asp?link=
Store [Date of access: 4.2.2016].

World Footwear: *World Footwear Yearbook 2015*,
URL: http://www.worldfootwear.com/
store.asp?link=Store [Date of access: 4.2.2016].

Yafasia: *Altkleidung Sammlung Schweiz divx.avi*,
Youtube.com 21.12.2011, URL: https://
www.youtube.com/watch?v=oTBYLDqvv1A [Date of
access: 7.12.2015].

Picture credits

- **Akash, GMB** (page 72)
- **Federal Archives, picture 105-DOA0179, photo: Walther Dobbertin, ca. 1906/1914** (page 23)
- **Caritas secondhand shop in Zurich** (page 91)
- **Umbrella organisation FairWertung e.V.** (page 88)
- **Hablützel, Adrian** (page 57)
- **Karim, Muhammad Mahdi 2009; www.micro2macro.net** (page 6)
- **Malefakis, Alexis 2012** (page 35)
- **Malefakis, Alexis 2016** (pages 13, 98, 101)
- **Reuben, Link 2011** (pages 14, 24, 25, 36, 50)
- **Reuben, Link 2012** (pages 28, 29)
- **Reuben, Link 2013** (pages 32, 39, 46, 52, 55, 59, 60)
- **Reuben, Link 2016** (pages 10, 20, 40, 43, 47, 51, 54, 65, 66, 69)
- **Texaid** (pages 84, 86, 87, 95)
- **Zhang Hongjin/Corbis** (page 79)